Starting School
The Vital Years

HENRY PLUCKROSE

SIMON & SCHUSTER
EDUCATION

© Henry Pluckrose 1993

First published in 1993 by Berghs Förlag AB, Stockholm
Revised and extended edition published in 1994 by Simon & Schuster Education
Campus 400, Maylands Avenue
Hemel Hempstead, Herts HP2 7EZ
United Kingdom

All rights reserved. No part of this publication may be reproduced, stored in a retrieval system, or transmitted in any form or by any means, electronic, mechanical, photocopying or otherwise, without the prior permission of the publisher.

British Library Cataloguing in Publication Data is available from the British Library

ISBN 0 7501 0673 5

Photoset in Palatino by
Derek Doyle & Associates, Mold, Clwyd.
Printed in Great Britain by
Redwood Books, Trowbridge

For Jan Källberg
Friend and colleague

An educated person is someone who asks questions, someone who thinks he doesn't know yet, someone who wants to learn more. Wendy Wasserstein, playwright.

Acknowledgements

I wish to record my thanks to the people who have helped in the preparation of this book:

Carl Hafström of the Swedish publisher Berghs Förlag for encouraging me to write it.

Hilary Devonshire of the Urban Learning Foundation, East London for her perceptive comments and suggestions.

Priscilla Benny (headteacher) and Margaret Grundy (member of staff) of Hugh Myddleton Infants School, London, for their suggestions and observations on record keeping.

Pauline Tambling of the Education Department of the Royal Opera House, London, for permission to include photographs taken at music workshops.

Ann Bickerstaffe for her careful preparation of the typescript and to all the young people with whom I work for continuing to demonstrate their unique ability to think and do.

Henry Pluckrose
London, Sofia and Stockholm
Spring 1994

The photographs on pages 68–9 by Leila Miller are reproduced by kind permission of the Royal Opera House, Education Department, Covent Garden.

Contents

Introduction 1

1 Being at school – the starting point 5

2 The early years at school – an analysis 11

3 But what are they going to do? 23

4 The classroom environment 35

5 Some days in school 47

6 The creative dimension 63

7 Being a teacher 75

8 The parental community 95

9 School and the young child 105

Appendix 111

Bibliography 115

Index 119

Starting School

Learning by doing. Hands on experience in a museum workshop

Introduction

We tried very hard but it seemed that every time we formed up into teams we would be reorganised.
  I was to learn later in life that we tend to meet any new situation by reorganisation; and a wonderful method it can be for creating the illusion of progress whilst producing confusion, inefficiency and demoralisation.
        CAIUS PATRONIUS, late of the Roman Legion, AD 65

This book has an unusual history. Over the past 25 years I have been fortunate to spend regular periods working with teachers in three very different countries – England, Sweden and Bulgaria. The text (extensively revised for English readers) draws upon these three cultures and seeks to show how the early years of schooling can be shaped to meet the needs of child, parent and teacher. To help those readers who are beginning a study of education, developments in educational practice and policy are set out below within an historical framework.

The Plowden Report

In England I taught through the 1960s and 1970s, a period when a real attempt was being made to establish primary schools which reflected young children's needs. The high point of this movement was marked by the publication, in 1966, of the Plowden Report which, had it been fully implemented, would have helped to create a climate in which the processes of learning and teaching could be critically examined.

This was not to be. Some of the fundamental restructuring recommended by the report was either ignored or only fitfully implemented, for example, the establishment of first and middle schools, and so the opportunity to extend the many initiatives which had been made in the most successful of our primary schools was lost. In this context it needs to be remembered that, at this time, the establishment of a clear image of what constituted a primary school was still at a comparatively experimental stage. Successive Hadow Reports, undertaken under the direction of The Board of Education, had concentrated upon the needs of adolescents (1926) the primary years (1931) and the children of infant and nursery age (1933). Although the passing of the *Education Act* of 1944 put into place a new structure for primary and secondary education and by so doing gave acknowledgement that primary education was to enjoy a unique place in state educational provision, economic restraints hampered its implementation. In 1949, for example, 36 per cent of children of secondary age were still taught in schools which also housed children of primary age.

The Plowden Report had therefore pointed to the direction in which English and Welsh primary schools should move. It put the child at the centre of the learning process and recommended the creation of a school-based curriculum that took into account the strengths and weaknesses – intellectual, social, emotional and physical – of each pupil. It was this emphasis which brought educationalists from all over the world to undertake study visits to schools which reflected the 'Plowden approach'.

Even though many of the recommendations of the Plowden Report were never to be adopted, its publication helped to focus attention upon the importance of the primary years.

The Plowden ideal, that of turning schools into learning centres rather than teaching shops cannot be judged as a failure since it was never fully implemented. A minority of schools – in areas like the West Riding of Yorkshire, Oxfordshire, Leicester, Berkshire and Bristol embraced a child centred approach with thought, planning and dedication. On the whole, however, in the great majority of primary classrooms, traditional methods continued to be used. Although members of the local inspectorate, advisory teachers and HMIs tried to develop a new methodology, their efforts were not marked by conspicuous success. Teachers on the whole were – and continue to be – traditional in their outlook. The inspiration which HMIs like Edith Biggs, Christian Schiller, who eventually became a lecturer at the London Institute of Education, and Tom Johns provided on in-service courses, the support given to innovative practices by Education Officers like Alec Clegg and Peter Newsam did little to change an educational policy still rooted in Victorian and Edwardian England.

Educational policy in the 1980s

In the 1980s, control of the educational system has been steadily taken from the local authorities and vested in agencies of central government. The bureaucracy that has resulted from this change has reduced the freedom that schools once had to plan their own curriculum, to establish their own approach to evaluation and teacher assessment and to draw freely upon services that were once available from their Local Education Authorities.

There is no doubt that the widely publicised collapse of one primary school, William Tyndale School, in Islington, North London, in the mid-1970s fuelled the political drive for fundamental changes in educational provision that culminated in the *Education Reform Act* of 1988. While the failure of this school provided impetus for educational retrenchment, the teachers' strikes of the 1980s seemed to project the message that teachers lacked professionalism and required the smack of firm government. Implicit in much of the propaganda which has surrounded the educational debates of the late 1980s and early 1990s is the message that the fundamental changes, made in recent years, are a direct consequence of the failures of the 1960s and the 1970s, which are projected as years of libertarianism and educational laissez-faire.

To correct these perceived 'errors', a back to basics policy has been steadily introduced: a tightly defined National Curriculum; testing: the publication of 'league' tables to indicate success (and failure); in-depth inspection of schools by lay inspectors as well as educationalists and a restructured teacher-training programme.

During visits abroad, in the 1980s, I was continually invited to address the same issues as were surfacing in England – but from a contrary standpoint.

'We have a National Curriculum. It is restrictive. It confines rather than releases ...'

'I'd love to involve my class around the work the archaeologists are doing in the village. But I can't. The historical period doesn't tie in with the curriculum.'

'I've 80 per cent immigrant children in my class. Somehow the curriculum goals don't fit their needs.'

Sadly these observations are very similar to those that I now hear in England and Wales.

In the rediscovered world of market forces, speed of change seems to be a key element. Unfortunately speed and effectiveness are not easy partners in areas of social policy. It is worth noting that the educational system which currently exists in Sweden was born of the *Education Act* of 1950. The passing of the Act was followed by 12 years of experimentation, consultation and preparation before all the changes were implemented and a new curriculum introduced (1962). After six years this curriculum was revised (1968) and was followed by a further fundamental re-shaping in 1980–81. Plans have been made for the presentation of a new curriculum in 1994–95.

It is interesting for us in England and Wales to compare this reflective approach with the many changes that have followed upon the passage of the *Education Reform Act* of 1988 culminating in the presentation, in Spring 1994, of a radically revised curriculum based on the report of a government committee chaired by Sir Ron Dearing.

New demands are being made of Swedish teachers and their pupils who will soon begin school at six rather than seven and these demands are echoed in other European countries. Bulgaria is looking to adopt a policy for schools that is less totalitarian, responsive to parental expectation and more able to meet the needs of children and their teachers. There too, similar questions are being asked: 'How do young children learn? How can teachers help children to grow and develop happily within the institution we call school?' These points were made even more forcibly by researchers in Sofia who were involved in a research project, *School for the twenty-first century:* 'We have to plan for tomorrow's children in tomorrow's world. In what ways can we help prepare our four, five and six-year-olds for such a challenge?'

It is important that a nation's children and their parents are not seen simply as insignificant pawns in a political process, whether the political inspiration for change comes from the right, left or centre of the political spectrum. In identifying the elements which we must continue to emphasise in our schools I am not suggesting that we return to the ideas of the 1960s or the 1970s. Our understanding has moved on with time. Nevertheless those of us who work with young children can draw upon sound educational practice (from whatever place and historical period) and apply it to the most unsatisfactory aspects of a National Curriculum, to revitalise learning, to link a child's home with school, and children and their parents with teachers.

1 Being at school – the starting point

The children in the classroom are much more important than are the subjects we would have them learn. From an educational seminar

In preparing this text I have been continually aware of the dangers that are implicit in putting educational thoughts into words. This book should not be seen as an academic script carved in stone and neatly parcelled into units suitable for learned discussions in colleges and universities. Essentially, it has been conceived as a notebook of ideas for anyone who is concerned with school programmes for the young in early childhood (parents, nursery and primary school teachers, students in training and teacher trainers).

The influence of the social and political climate on educational ideas

My personal interest in teachers, teaching and school organisation has taken me to many different countries and cultures throughout the world and to many educational institutions of various kinds within the British Isles. In each of them, politicians, academics, teachers and, to some extent, parents seek to implement an educational methodology which complements and fits comfortably within its current social and political climate. Many examples could be used to illustrate this phenomenon. The response of the Government of the United States to Russia's success in space exploration in the 1960s was to elevate the place of science in schools and to downgrade the place of the creative arts. Similarly the 'back-to-basics' movement which spread across Western Europe (including Britain) in the late 1980s and early 1990s has been based not upon statistical evidence that more informal methods have failed but partly upon the premise that a mere formal educational diet is cheaper to deliver than one which takes into account the individual needs of the teacher and the taught.

Thus a sovereign state may be liberal and gently paternalistic, tightly totalitarian or organise itself somewhere between these two extremes. The schools that are established within it will tend to reflect their political stance. We could therefore ask whether the child starting school within any society is seen as a unit to be shaped to meet the demands of a predetermined political plan or as an individual with unique potential. It is because the education of the young is a political issue that there is no universal agreement as to how best to prepare children for the adult world. One nation will insist that its teachers deliver a clearly defined, age-related curriculum package. Another will prefer to support a curriculum that is locally determined and largely classroom led. In the first model, subjects are clearly listed and teaching hours specified. In the second, the time spent on each subject area is left to the discretion of the teacher. The first model implies that teachers cannot be trusted to deliver a well conceived learning programme to the children in their care, while the second carries the message that teachers are regarded by their society as competent, trained professionals. Implicit in these observations is the importance of the school curriculum, for it gives messages about how a society values its children and the teachers and other professionals who work in its schools.

The individual at the centre of the learning process

The areas explored in the pages which follow have been largely determined by the experience I have had of working with children. Over a period of twenty years, first as deputy headteacher and then as headteacher, I learned, not just from books and lectures, but from first hand experience, a little of how young children see their world and how they respond to it; of their needs, for example, for play, security, affection, direction, and support; of their independence; of their approach to problem solving, and of their ways of thinking. I came to realise, at first reluctantly, but then with growing certainty, that many of the structures we build around our children in organised institutions are, at their best, largely ineffective and, at their worst, positively destructive. We need to halt the rush towards formalised training and ask (as every educator should do daily) 'What does this child need of me? How can I help him (or her) handle the excitement, fears, joys and anticipations of childhood?

In the London school, where I was headteacher for 18 years, learning was paramount. We had, as do all teachers working within the state system, the responsibility of providing an environment in which young children could confront reading, writing, mathematics and the usual range of school subjects. Equally important was our need to relate these demands to the emotional, social, intellectual and physical level of each of our children. It was as important for us to create a society in school in which children grew happily, as it was for us to create one in which they grew intellectually.

The teaching staff with whom I worked, each responsible for a group of 30 or more children, quickly realised that academic ability had little to do with age. Being five or six years of age bore no relationship to specific levels of achievement: the state of 'fiveness' or 'sixness' was no guide at all to a child's ability to jump over an externally devised, predetermined educational hurdle (like being able to count to 100, write a sentence or know that 9×2 always made 18). There were some four-year-olds who joined the school as fluent readers; there were others, like Jessica a four and a half-year-old with a measured reading age of over eight, who needed only a modicum of help in the process of decoding words; some children, like Patrick, struggled to master print and even when they were eight years of age continued to be hesitant when confronted with an unfamiliar book or a previously unseen page.

It would have been easy to ignore the latent abilities of the children with whom we worked and assume that at five (or six) each child would be delivered to the school as an academically empty bottle waiting to be filled within a predetermined time scale to an adult devised formulae – an assumption that would have led to a system that measured each child against a set of criteria rather than against his or her own growth and development. Such a system would have condemned Patrick to receiving special treatment because he was a slow reader at nine (even though he could follow diagrams, bleed car brakes and change a car wheel) and 'forget' Jessica because she, as a fluent reader could largely be ignored until other children 'caught her up'.

We realised that for a school to succeed for all the pupils we needed to create a framework that was centred upon the uniquely personal knowledge and experience of each child (even though that child might be only four or five years-of-age). It is to such personally 'owned' knowledge that new knowledge can be attached.

The proposition that, each five or six-year-old is a unique individual with a personal body of knowledge that can provide an effective school-based learning programme might initially seem too ambitious to contemplate – let alone deliver. Can we, however, afford to be so doubting?

Time and learning

Time is largely meaningless to children; their emotional, intellectual, social and physical growth is personal; and their experience of life egocentric. The attempt, therefore, to classify children by their age alone is full of pitfalls. Is it possible for a teacher, headteacher, politician or administrator to group children by 'fiveness', 'sixness' or even 'tenness' if the path that each child has taken to reach that point is so very different?

The six-year-old from Somalia, a refugee adopted by a kindly Swedish family had, in those few years, experienced more trauma and pain than someone ten times her age. She had experienced and learned, at first hand, about death, starvation, cruelty, poverty and – in contrast about the abundance of food, warmth, love and compassion shown by her adopted parents. The five-year-old who has grown up in a loving caring family may have developed a rich spoken language which allows her to express ideas and thoughts far more sophisticated than those of her peer group. The six-year-old who has spent much of his time playing in the woods, lakes and streams around his home in the countryside will intuitively bring to school greater feeling for the ebb and flow of the natural seasons than a child whose early years has been spent in the drab back streets of an inner city or in institutional care.

Some years ago, in Sofia, a prominent educationalist asked me in a television interview at what age children should start school. For example, 'Can children start school at six? Is it possible?' This is very similar to the question I am most frequently asked in Sweden where the school starting age will be lowered over the next few years. 'What can we do about children who are not yet ready to begin school? Starting school at seven seems to be successful. Why should we try to lower it?'

Both questions begin from a false premise. Age is not the factor that should determine school entry, for it should not be the sole basis for the programme that is to be followed there. The questions, pertinent though they are, needed to be rephrased and extended. 'These young people happen to be about five or six years of age. They are going to enter a place where their knowledge and understanding is to be deepened and extended. What do we need to know about these new members of our school community? How can we build upon what they know already? What do they need of us – as individuals and as a group?'

It is to such considerations that we will now turn.

2 The early years at school – an analysis

The search for wisdom begins with wonder.   ARISTOTLE

It is difficult to remember what it was like to be five, six or seven. Looking back, I have a hazy recollection of those early days of schooling. In my memory the classroom was large and overflowing with children. The desks were small, the teacher tall and severe, there was a distinctive smell (a mixture of bodies and the oil with which the school keeper treated the wooden floor) and I had a pencil which never quite did what I expected of it. When, recently, I peered into that classroom of my memories little had changed. The room still looked cramped, even though tables had replaced the iron desks. There was still a chalkboard and a teacher's table. Growing bodies and minds were still squeezed into the box we call a classroom. What was new!

Perhaps such memories and, through them, a fleeting return to our own past help focus upon the issue central to this book. Our children are powerless, faced as they are with the restraints of a world not their making. The English poet, John Wayne, recalls this early period of his life very dramatically. In his poem 'The Demagogue' he tells his long dead teacher 'You lay across my childhood like a stone.'

To prevent future poets from such bitter recriminations, we must redress the balance and begin to value childhood. To do this, we need to reflect on the nature of the young child alongside whom we are privileged to live and work. Let me then, try to create a word picture of this fascinating creature.

Perceptions

The most obvious characteristic of the four, five or six-year-old is the joy that comes from movement, the delight in using all the senses (not just those of sight and hearing) in the personal quest to unravel the confusions within a personal world. Is this so very different from us? A few days before writing this chapter I visited the city of Bath in south west England. Bath has a long history. The Romans built a settlement around a hot spring and erected a temple over a site which had been considered sacred long before the Romans arrived. When the Roman Empire fell, the hot springs remained and have been visited through the intervening centuries by the sick and suffering who came to seek relief from their pain.

The ruins of the Roman bath still stand. Tourists come to wonder at the architecture, pausing perhaps to think of times past. They stand and gaze at the steaming water, sniff the damp, musty air, listen to the rush of the spring as it bursts through the earth and touch the stones. Notices warn them not to taste the water. It is rather hot and not too clean. But the reason for such warnings is clear, for even adults seek a total experience. Simply seeing or listening is not enough.

And so it is with children. Touching, hearing, tasting, smelling and seeing play a central part in the way they accumulate knowledge. A visit to a farm with a group of five-year-olds will produce as many comments about the smell of pig, goat and cow as it will about the softness of a lamb's coat or the warmth of freshly given milk. If both adults and children learn best when their senses are totally involved, it is clear that we should try to ally the senses to the activities which children undertake in school.

In passing, I should observe that young children seem to be more in harmony with messages received through their senses than are adults. It is as though the child's senses have not been dimmed and diminished by age or impoverished through neglect. For the growing child the world *is* a wonder-full place. 'Have you felt how hot the sun is?' a five-year-old remarked to me. An everyday observation, except that her question was triggered by the warmth of the grass into which she was pressing her hand. Such heightened perception is obvious in artists, poets and musicians and, when we meet it in adults, we remark upon it. Yet children possess it to a remarkable degree. Sadly it does not stay long. There is little place for sense or sensitivity in the mdoern school curriculum.

Movement

Children seem driven by a need to move. Indeed the typical six-year-old is possessed of an inexhaustible supply of energy. Unless totally engaged in an activity, whether building with bricks or watching a cow give birth, a six-year-old seems to find it almost impossible to be still. In part, this physical activity reflects a need to understand his or her environment. At sixteen months old, Peter struggles to his feet, takes a timid step and falls. The process is continually repeated, despite failure and pain, until the hesitant steps become confident ones, until walking becomes running, running becomes jumping, kicking, climbing, balancing – until the challenge his world presents is met, faced and conquered.

Throughout their primary years, children continue to meet physical challenges. The co-ordination necessary to catch and throw a ball, to skip, tie a knot, draw a line with ruler and pencil, ride a bike, lock a seat belt, manipulate the controls of a video or television set, fit pieces of Lego together or feed a disk into a computer are all aspects of a growing ability to come to terms with the complexities of living. This need to make demands of their bodies should not be frustrated or ignored. If it is, those of us who work with young children know all too well what happens. Their frustration is marked with unhappiness and anger.

An English educationalist, Susan Isaacs, writing in the 1930s, observed that working with young children was like living alongside 'little moments of explosion'. In giving advice to a young lady who planned to enter a training college for teachers she observed, 'Take four five-year-olds on a train journey from Paddington to Penzance. If you manage to leave the train smiling and content you'll make a teacher.' 'Moments of explosion' on a seven-hour journey by steam train can be difficult to live with. Like fireworks, the explosions can be beautiful, creative and stimulating. Like fireworks they can be handled badly. When this happens the explosions cause pain to all those unfortunate enough to be close at hand.

Fortunately young children are able to harness their tremendous physical energy. They are makers and doers and draw upon a rich imagination to create in conventional as well as in less traditional ways. Whether shaping clay into a rough pot, digging and moulding wet sand, fashioning a car from a cornflakes box or making a doll from the tube at the centre of a toilet roll, Mary and Alpha are using physical skills to explore their world. The involvement is active and demands, for success, a harmony of brain, eye and hand.

Making and doing does not just involve things and objects. Young children match, in imagination, the models they see in real life. In Belgrade I watched a six-year-old dress up as a partisan fighter and re-live stories of his grandfather's bravery in the Second World War (not so different from child dramas which continue to be played out in the backstreets of Belfast and in the townships of the West Bank). Fortunately the models are not always bleak. I remember, happily, those moments when my young son role-played the man whose lorry cleaned the drains and when my small daughters prepared their dolls for a visit to the dentist. In such 'games' children play-out their hopes, fears, perceptions, anxieties. Their matching of the society in which they are growing up helps them to come to terms with it and (for better or for worse) to respond to its strains and tensions.

I have observed active, imaginative physical play in many cultures and in many different settings. One of my earliest memories of Sweden is of watching a three-year-old French girl sing and dance like a pop star. She was standing on a rock overlooking Lake Maleren. There was no audience – just me, an unseen observer. Who has not wondered at the unexpected perception shown by children as they act out the roles of mother and father or (even more professionally devastating) of teachers and children? A little Chinese girl in Hong Kong tearfully told me that she couldn't go on being a teacher. The children (a motley collection of soft toys) wouldn't sit up straight, fold their arms and answer politely.

Curiosity

Movement, so central to being five, six or seven, is further stimulated by a curiosity which seems limitless. The 'Why', 'What', 'When', 'How', 'Where' questions of early childhood grow in intensity and broaden to take in both the obvious and the superficially bizarre. Questions seem to tumble out one after another.

> 'Why are my eyes brown?'
> 'What makes a giraffe have a long neck?'
> 'Do angels wear shoes?'
> 'How does a bee *know* he's a bee and not a wasp?'
> 'Can ants talk to other ants?'
> 'What happens when I flush the toilet?'
> 'Do you believe in God?'
> 'Where was I before I was me?'
> 'Are there dinosaurs in the Bible?'

Essentially abstract questions are as common as ones which follow upon things seen, touched, smelt, heard and tasted.

The answers we give to such questions helps give shape and form to a complex and confusing world. We (like a child) can only ask a question about something of which we know at least a little. For example how many questions can you or I ask about quantum physics without some awareness of what it is?

When six-year-old Maria asks 'Is there a God?' she is telling me, the adult listener, that she has heard of somebody who is called 'God' and that some people believe that there is a spiritual dimension beyond the physical world. This thought might not be expressed as clearly as mine. Her thoughts – at six – are likely to be more hazy, less defined. Yet my answer will provide further shape to her understanding, enabling her to refine the next question she asks about the subject whether this question is asked immediately or in six-months' time.

It is because children's observations indicate their awareness, perception and understanding that we should treat their questions with respect and try to ensure that the answers we give relate to the maturity of the questioner. Aidan, at six, asked me to explain negative number (-1, -2, etc.). 'You know,' he said 'the numbers on the other side of zero.' I was forced to reply as I might have done had he been twice his age. He was curious about numbers. He was fascinated in the idea of numbers 'beyond zero', his question demanded a reply *appropriate to his level of understanding*. My answer left him temporarily satisfied. A few days later he returned to ask me if negative numbers could be multiplied and divided. He seemed to assume that they could be used for addition and substraction! Perhaps this is why a Chinese philosopher observed that thinking involves asking one's own questions, not answering those of other people!

Curiosity and questioning (and the langauge which develops through it) are key elements in personal learning. A five-year-old holds the pair of knitted bootees she wore as a baby. 'I wore these when I was small.' The questions which followed might have been asked by an academic historian. 'What did I look like then? Did we live in the same house as we do now? Did you wear boots like this when you were a baby?' The concepts of time and place, continuity and change, similarity and difference are implicit in these questions. Curiosity (allied to a rapidly expanding vocabulary) provides a perfect base for learning. If the material which is being learned is appropriate, assimilation seems to be almost effortless.

Play

All the characteristics which I have listed so far are embraced within one activity which is central to childhood, an activity I have already touched upon. It is the activity we call play.

Children as players have long fascinated both philosophers and educationalists. Aristotle and Plato both insisted that it was an essential stage in human development: Darwin in the *'Origin of Species'* (1859) tied play into his general theory of survival believing it to be a 'manifestation of encoded instincts'; Sigmund Freud (1856–1939) regarded play as a form of therapy which gave the 'young player' the opportunity of re-ordering events, circumstances and people into new patterns in which he or she could feel secure.

In recent times, Jean Piaget (1896–1980) has contributed much to our understanding of the significance of play in the intellectual development of children. His research suggests that play (and the learning processes which accompany it) follows a specific and predictable pattern in all children. Piaget classified this pattern, though it is important to remember that since consecutive stages merge and overlap, the classification serves only to indicate a process of development and is not tightly age specific.

Piaget's analysis

Simple motor play
The first stage of simple motor play or sensorimotor thought occurs in the early stages of development, approximately between 0–2 years. At this stage, information about the world is gathered through the senses and processed through images and memory. This can be observed in an eighteen-month-old child at play. Notice how much physical contact occurs. A wooden toy car is as likely to be rubbed against the ear or put into the mouth as it is to be pushed across the floor. Indeed when the toy is not in the hand or close to the body it seems no longer to be regarded as a play thing.

The pre-operational stage
This next stage (approximately between the ages of 2 and 7 years) is marked by tremendous outbursts of energy in which information about the world obtained through the senses is reprocessed within a broader context through the use of language (the how, what, why

mentioned earlier in this chapter). A characteristic of this level of development is *animism*, a term used to describe the difficulty which children at this stage, have of thinking logically. Let me illustrate this with an example. Patrick, aged five, attended a school play presented by a touring theatre company. The actors, who retold the story of Hansel and Gretel, used a PE cupboard in the school hall as a dressing room. It was from this cupboard that the witch emerged and into which she disappeared at the end of the play. The teacher jokingly observed at the end of the performance that the cupboard was a very useful place – now there was a witch inside to watch for naughty children. Although Patrick met the actors in their everyday clothes after the performance, the cupboard became a frightening place for him, even though he knew it to be empty. The weeks after the performance were marked by nightmares and fear of the dark. The reason for this only became clear when, some months later, Patrick saw a bonfire and remarked, 'The witch is all burned up now, isn't she?' It was only then that he told his father the story of the actress and the broom cupboard. In passing, it is worth noting that Patrick destroyed the witch by employing imagination, which at this stage of development is vivid.

It is important for those who work with young children to appreciate that the significance of Piaget's 'pre-operational' classification, for the implication of child as learner, are profound. If we accept that the young learners' perceptions are limited to what is conveyed through the senses, and are used in the construction of idiosyncratic interpretation, it becomes much clearer to us, as teachers, that teaching and learning is not one single unified process. Piagetian research, for example, suggests that many children find it difficult to grasp the concept of distance – that an aircraft high in the sky, where it looks small, has the same dimensions as an identical plane on an airport runway, where it looks very large.

This inability to conceptualise can cause considerable confusion to the young learner and provide a very uneasy base on which to build further. Rosaline, aged six, was told in class about global warming. She was told of the polar ice caps ('great mountains of ice'). She was told the ice would melt, something which she had observed when ice is put in summer drinks. Her question, 'What will we do when the ice melts and everybody drowns?' indicates something of how children think at this stage of their development – and by implication the care with which we as teachers should take in our presentation of new knowledge.

The operational stage
At the operational stage of thinking (approximately between the ages of 8 and 12 years) the world slowly becomes more comprehensible. Past knowledge is continually being re-shaped against present experience. At this stage children begin to group and classify their experience – by one or more variables and by function and begin to become intellectually discreet. As this process develops fantasy and make believe become less important.

The concrete operational stage
Concrete operational can be considered as a sub-heading of the operational stage. At this level children have the ability to think in concrete terms but have problems dealing with abstractions. For example a nine-year-old may be able to grasp that King Alfred deserved the criticism of the widow whose cakes he allowed to burn but have no understanding of why the story is told, which is as an illustration of the worries and concerns of kingship in ninth-century Britain.

The formal operational stage
Piaget classified his final stage as one of formal operational thinking (the age of 12 upwards). Here we have thinking at its most sophisticated and complex – the ability to think in an abstract way without the necessity of concrete reference points, for example, the handling of algebraic equations or speculation about what might happen if ....

Although it is only the second stage of Piaget's classification which concerns us here, his analysis is significant to everyone who works with young children. Piaget saw play as an indicator of a child's intellectual development. By appreciating the stage at which a child is functioning, it becomes possible for the teacher to devise situations in which learning can be effective and appropriate (and by implication, pleasant and non-stressful).

To summarise, Piaget argued that the basis of understanding stems from a continual interaction between the outside world and the ideas each individual holds at any one moment. Children (like adults) bring meaning to the world (that is, construct theories) through this active interaction. Personal understanding therefore comes as new experience and so builds onto, and clarifies, the sum of all past experience.

Piaget's research encouraged many other psychologists to reflect on the process of learning. Among the most influential of these was David Ausubel, quoted in Curzon D. (1985), who investigated the way in which concepts were learned. Like Piaget he noted that past knowledge shaped present understanding and, that if learning was to be meaningful, learners needed to do more than simply repeat what they had just been told or rephrase things they had just read. It therefore follows that core learning, on which so many school programmes are based, is not likely to help the learner to develop thinking skills. Ausubel suggested that, from birth, children are engaged in building knowledge 'frameworks' from their personal observations of the regularities of the events and situations which they meet in everyday life ... that a ball when thrown into the air always falls to the ground; that a stone tossed into water always sinks. This remorseless accumulation of observations (interpreted but not always understood) has tremendous bearing upon subsequent learning. As Ausubel observed, 'The most important single factor influencing learning is what the learner already knows. Ascertain that and teach accordingly.'

Of course, we should not regard a particular analysis as a final model. The examples examined above serve to stress the importance of play as an indicator of the development of thinking. One might say that the research described above confirms the observations of generations of philosophers:

> 'Humans are truly human only when they play.' J. C. F. von Schiller (1759–1805)

> 'Play is the natural state of children. When not asleep they are in motion, active, in play.' Fredrick Froebel (1782–1852)

> 'Play is children's way of perceiving the world that they have been called upon to change.' Maxim Gorki (1868–1936).

Caldwell Cook, a teacher in The Perse School, Cambridge, wrote a book describing the methods he employed in his classroom. In *The Playway*, which was first published in 1919 and regularly reprinted until 1948, Cook showed that, by linking the children's natural desire to 'find out' alongside their natural desire to play, the classroom could become a place of mutual respect, co-operation and learning. Cook saw play as any activity 'you do with your whole heart', a definition which blurs the line between work (with its protestant overtones of harshness) and play (so often judged to be time wasting and therefore worthless).

I have dealt at some length with the implications of learning and playing and with the child as a player because it is vital that this characteristic be taken into account when thinking about the education provision we need to make for children in the age group four to eight. Thus applying Cook's definition of play, our five or six-year-old might learn about capacity by 'playing' with water or sand using a range of containers (each of a different standard measure); he or she might 'learn' about numbers 'by playing' with mathematical apparatus which directs the player to an understanding of the nature of the number 10 (see pages 38–9). Similarly appreciation of language could be developed through rhymes, songs and simple drama, approached through 'play' with puppets and toy theatres, or science through experimenting ('playing') with magnets or simple electrical circuits. The continuing success and popularity of hands-on museums like the Science Museum in London with its children's rooms seem to confirm Cook's analysis.

Play, then, is a means by which children come to terms with and develop an understanding of the world in which they are living. It is a social activity in which the child may play as an individual in the company of adults or his or her peer groups or together with other children. The social and cultural setting in which play takes place will influence the nature of the play and the learning which comes from the experience. 'Playing out' a security incident in Belfast, or Sarajevo with a group of friends, carries with it implicit attitudes which may harden in later life; just as playing with 'Lego' may provide valuable insight (to be subsequently drawn upon) into the way in which technical and constructional problems may be resolved.

Play involves activity. When young children are allowed and encouraged to become active agents in their own learning they reveal a characteristic which might otherwise be overlooked – responsibility. It is so easy to swamp a child with rules (spoken and implied) that self-responsibility is never given opportunity to flower. When this over direction happens, the child becomes little more than a living package to be manipulated by well intentioned adults.

Children are capable of taking on responsibilities within the classroom at an early stage in their school life. These responsibilities will relate both to the care of personal possessions but also to the care of the room itself. Responsibilities for the appearance of the library shelves, the cleanliness of the painting materials, the tidiness of display tables, the watering of flowers and plants, the neatness of toys and equipment should be devolved upon individual children. This will confirm that the teacher trusts the children in his or her care and acknowledges that growth brings with it both privilege and responsibility. It will also confirm that the classroom belongs to both teacher and taught.

This moving, talking, playing, responsible, active, learning, questioning and curious human being has one further characteristic which must be mentioned. The child needs the security which can only be given by a caring adult.

The need for security

Anyone who works with young children is aware of their potential. For this potential to be fully realised, the child needs to feel safe. Safety for a six-year-old means having an adult near by who can be trusted, who is consistent and fair in dealing with each child. We, as adults (be we parents or teachers), continually signal our expectations to the children with whom we live. These signals can as easily dampen growth as encourage it.

The personal path to knowledge

Life is a paradox of continuation and re-creation. We grow, we change and yet we are the same. Learning is like life. All that happens to Peter or Ella, Tipu or Sandra *now* is a prelude to their individual tomorrows. All that happened in their personal pasts has been but a prelude to their present.

If we can accept that every child takes a personal path towards knowing, knowledge and understanding and at the same time each child has characteristics which are commonly shared, school can be the adventure it ought to be.

In the early years of schooling children are truly alive!

3 But what are they going to do?

What does it mean to be a child and what do children think about in the classroom?

The question that has most commonly been put to me by teachers over the past twenty-five years is, 'Can you please help me. I've got a class of 30 children aged .... Here is the school curriculum. What shall I *do* with them?'

What should I *do* with them? (Notice the emphasis.) My response is invariably to challenge the assumptions which underlie the question. Surely it is not I, the teacher, who should be thinking about *doing*? Would it not be more appropriate to consider the individuals who make up the class?

How children learn

This shifting of emphasis has dramatic and far reaching implications. I, the teacher, become less of a stage director and more of a stage hand, helping each child to play their part in the theatre which we call classroom. Learning, growth, the struggle towards social acceptance and the battle to overcome personal inadequacy takes place inside each child *as an individual*, not within a collective (however well that collective be run, however benign its director, however sympathetic and loving the adults who organise its programme).

This view of the worth of the individual has been cleverly and clearly explored by the Canadian academic, Robertson Davies. In a series of acclaimed novels, published in 1983, 1989 and 1991, Davies builds on the idea that throughout life each individual is an actor, not just a player but the principal in the play (be it comedy or tragedy) which is their life. Those who, for a while, share the drama with them (parents, teachers, employers and shop assistants, even eventually their own children) are bit-players, passing, ephemeral. It may be that

Shakespeare had a similar thought when he observed that:

> 'All the world's a stage
> And all the men and women merely players ...' (*As you like it*, Act II, Scene 7)

It is interesting to note that contemporary European academics have expressed almost identical ideas. James Britton, an English educationalist, expressed the importance of 'I' in the learning process as follows: 'Our educational plans *must* take into account the person, the unit in the network of human relations, the "I" that reacts to experience, acts, suffers, learns and goes on expecting.'

The Italian Pietro Prini is more romantic but just as direct when he states that every child, every person must obtain a view of himself, shaped by personal experiences 'within the mind'.

Whether we accept this viewpoint in whole or in part the young learner who provides the focus for this book is certainly egocentric. His or her world is limitless, the future unimaginable. This said, the demand which such an interpretation of children's needs places upon the teacher must – at first sight – appear impossible to meet. How can one adult simultaneously satisfy, in one small space, the physical, emotional, intellectual and social needs of 30 children?

To answer such a question it is necessary to return to first principles.

An appropriate curriculum

We could, of course, begin by constructing a beautiful curriculum, write it down, bind it within expensive covers and print it in great quantities for all to see. This proclamation of intention is fine and appropriate if we assume that the children who are to follow it are little better than thoughtless robots. Fortunately for us (but unfortunately for government policy-makers and their curriculum designers), our children are vibrant and alive who when bored (rather like us) turn their minds to other things.

Alternatively we could begin by trying to identify those elements which are an integral part of every effective learning programme. If, once identified, we construct a curriculum around these elements, *the process of learning* can become its driving force. Compare this with the model described in the preceding paragraph where input (knowledge) is the raison d'etre for the curriculum and its delivery. 'This is what children shall know at five or six or seven because we, the adults, ordain it.'

And so, ignoring for a moment the question of input of knowledge let us consider briefly the feelings which a practical curriculum should generate in the learner.

A feeling of positive achievement

Hopefully each and every child should be able to look back on a school week and feel that something has been achieved. Thus the five-year-old who can already form her letters should not have her time wasted by being made 'to learn' to write, the six-year-old who can add and subtract numbers up to 100 should not be invited to do page upon page of addition and subtraction sums simply because his friend Peter needs the practice. Both of these examples (and I could give many others) stem from the desire, as one young teacher told me, 'to keep the group together' (that is, it's better for some children to stand still academically than to encourage academic divergence). Surely an effective curriculum will relate to the individual and not collective needs, to the individual and not to an 'average'.

A feeling of pleasure from learning

In this context I am reminded of the five-year-old who remarked to his father after four days in school 'I've tried it. I've done it. Is it going to be like this for the rest of the year? If it is do I have to go tomorrow?'

It is sad when children respond to school in such a way. Thirsty for knowledge which they can assimilate if well presented, a diet of formal exercises delivered in neat 40-minute packets have little appeal to growing minds for it ignores the way in which young people learn.

Can we expect anybody to learn effectively if the learning process is dulling, boring, stultifying. I am not here recommending that 'fun' and 'happiness' become core units in the curriculum! To make knowledge your own requires application and diligence on the part of the learner. What I *am* suggesting is that these qualities are much more likely to be in evidence when the learner is aware of the progress being made.

A feeling of challenge

Much of the knowledge we make our own has its roots in the

challenge of finding out, through satisfying a personal curiosity, from discovering for oneself. We should not limit the six-year-old's quest for information simply because certain knowledge is deemed (by an expert) to be more appropriate to a subsequent school year. A six-year-old may be curious about Queen Elizabeth I, 'The Armada' or the England of Robin Hood, life in the coal mines when grandpa worked in one, Viking longships, number patterns in the 100 square, painting with acrylic colours and a palette knife or setting up a simple weaving loom. The acquisition of such personal knowledge and skills is to be fostered and encouraged. Six-year-old Mirjam who becomes fascinated with life 'long ago' as a result of visiting standing stones in Angelsey is not going to use her knowledge to undermine her teacher when 'Early People in Wales' becomes the class topic. Mirjam will be able to bring to her future work an enthusiasm, which has already been kindled, an interest which is already alight. Those who teach must try to avoid seeing knowledge in tight packets, the packets themselves shaped by the text books which we depend upon for the context of our lessons. How much more successful will our teaching be if we can help each child to follow a study at his or her own level!

Again I must clarify this observation. George Rupp, President of Rice University was quoted in *The New York Times* of 1 December 1992 as saying: 'Knowledge is consistently escalating. We no longer have any easy limits to set around what we ought to know'. It follows that while it is difficult to frame a school curriculum, it is essential that children be introduced to an ever expanding corpus of knowledge. The adult cannot just sit back and wait for children to indicate their interests, or for personal discovery to dominate the school programme. Let me illustrate this point with a simple example. A globe is brought into the classroom and becomes a focus for discussion. Each child is faced with a difficult concept. The world as we see it appears to be flat. But really the world is a sphere. Its surface is covered with more water than land .... Each child will add the new information to that which they already possess. It is the impact of the new information which generates personal enquiry. The word discovery in an educational context should therefore not be taken to mean that every bit of learning is originated by the learner. We cannot afford to wait for every child to discover that the world is round.

A feeling of individual worth

Every child should feel that he or she is an individual with unique interests, feelings, ideas and skills. This is but an extension of my point above. The activities offered to young learners should be sufficiently varied and sufficiently stimulating to draw upon the individual gifts of each child. 'Alan is good at reading', said Elsa. 'He can read the words and I'll make the puppets move. My fingers go better than his.' Young children quickly become aware of the particular accomplishments of their classmates. Such gifts must not be allowed to atrophy and die.

In the school where I was headteacher, many six and seven-year-olds were introduced to the violin. To watch their tiny fingers moving over the strings of a quarter-size violin was for me, an adult who had grown up as a cathedral chorister, quite awe-inspiring. Children can master sophisticated skills. My granddaughter's nursery school was equipped with three computers and supporting educational software. The users were three and four-year-olds, not the teachers. Why are our expectations so geared to everyday mediocrity?

A feeling of safety and trust

Young children, new to school, require a firm base from which to explore the things which the classroom has to offer. This security is enhanced when the teacher has a clear idea of the organisation which is necessary to underpin his or her work and is sufficiently confident to share these strategies with the children.

In one school in which I worked the six-year-olds spent some moments at the end of each day discussing how the next school day would begin. In this short discussion period the teacher listened to the children and, from it, determined which of the children had paintings to finish, who was to spend time cooking, clean the rabbit's hutch or complete an unfinished piece of writing. She also told the children of her requirements – indicating which children she needed to hear read, teach numbers and so on. This shared 'deciding-time' was a feature of the school day. If Mrs Phipps, the teacher, was absent the children could, and did, 'run themselves'. Their phrase, 'We always do it like this', indicated children who were competent organisers. They were able to organise because the organisation meant something *to them*.

A feeling of caring, and acceptance

Implicit in every learning programme are values, some explicit, some hidden. Learners (be they six or sixty years of age) are adept at identifying the things which the teacher seems to value. When we take a child's painting and pin it crookedly to a wall what message are we giving about how we value the painting and about how we value the visual appearance of the classroom? When we ignore the fact that Andrea is bored with the activity we have forced her to undertake, even though she has consistently shown that her abilities transcend it, what are we saying about the way we value her intelligence? When we dismiss a whispered fear as childish, or an anxiety as unnecessary, how successful are we being at grasping what it is to be growing up in a rapidly changing world?

These sentiments, which lie at the very heart of my ideal learning programme, can be expressed in another way – that the curriculum should help the young child towards self-awareness, self-confidence, self-esteem, self-discipline and self-criticism. During the early years of school, only a start can be made towards the setting of the twin goals of autonomy and self-knowing. Yet it is because the first years of school life provide an important signpost to the future, that the curriculum (all that happens in a school day, a school week, a school year in the classroom, the dining room and the playground) must be appropriately conceived and delivered.

In an address given in the late 1960s, Sir Alec Clegg, a much respected British educationalist, suggested that the programmes that were being implemented in the primary schools of the local education authority for which he was responsible, sought to do one thing: 'To enable each child to enter a personal future with firm steps and clear eyes'.

A poetic dream, perhaps, but a dream which is appropriate to all the young people in our care. Of course we cannot, as teachers or head teachers, ignore the restraints imposed upon us by government legislation, the specific demands of our school curriculum and the particular profile of the school in which we work. What we can do, however, is to take such framework as is imposed and enrich it, re-shape it and present it within a programme which is appropriate and meaningful for the children who undertake it.

Throughout all that I have written in these pages, the teacher is presented as someone who lives and learns alongside the young people for whom he or she is responsible. As interpreter of the curriculum, the teacher is someone who understands that children need to go and do, to talk, discover, participate and contribute, to create in words, music, movement and the visual arts, use modern technology (such as computers) and present their findings in all manner of ways (words written and spoken, pictures, plays, diagrams and graphs).

This accepted, a central question remains. How can the principal components of the programme of study that the children are to undertake be identified. The strands in the following table present themselves (and are to be found in the formal written curriculum of schools across the Western world).

The principal components of a programme of study

Language

A deepening and extending of language through:

1. Stories, rhymes and poetry.
2. The application of the spoken word to a variety of situations – descriptions, story telling, the exploration of more abstract ideas and concepts, simple drama.
3. An introduction to ways of recording ideas on paper (writing).
4. Interpreting the printed word (reading).
5. Learning how to listen.

Mathematics

An approach to mathematics through work with a wide range of apparatus (see Chapter 4); findings to be recorded (in a range of different ways) as and when appropriate.

Thematic studies

An introduction to scientific, geographic, historical and cultural studies through themes or topics, incorporating language and mathematical elements as and when appropriate.

The Arts

1 Exploration of a wide range of picture making materials (see Chapter 4).
2 Three-dimensional model making using clay, junk material of all kinds and wood.
3 Music making through song and tuned percussion instruments. Listening to music of all kinds, from folk to classical.
4 Drama. Puppetry. Creative movement and simple folk dances.
5 Beyond the classroom. Visiting museums, watching live theatre.

Free play

Both inside and outside the classroom (see Chapter 4).

Motor-skill development

Through games and gymnastic activities develop skills such as balance, jumping, landing at speed, catching, throwing, handling bats, sticks, hoops and so on.

Practical skills

An introduction to equipment – the computer keyboard, the camera and the tape recorder.

Social skills

Running throughout the type of programme outlined above will be a common strand – the development of social skills. If the social cohesion of the group is unsatisfactory a number of areas could be examined. The questions I would ask myself at this point might be:

- Is the programme challenging enough?
- Is it too challenging?
- Are my expectations appropriate to the needs of the children in my care?
- Have I clearly signalled my goals?
- Am I sufficiently aware of the *abilities* (not the problems!) of the children with whom I am working?
- Am I taking into account the economic and cultural backgrounds of the children? (How do Muslim children interpret my Britishness, my language,

my culture? How can I best respond to theirs?)
- Am I giving children enough time to show social grace or is the day too fragmented and subject-dominated?

Implementation

Let us now consider how such an ambitious programme might be delivered bearing in mind that we are seeking to help children to become independent and self-motivated. I do not imagine, for example, that every child will necessarily be following the same part of the programme at the same time (for flexibility in the use of time will result in flexibility in output).

Entry into almost every element in the menu I have outlined above could be made through a broadly thematic approach. The theme followed might be dictated by the curriculum designer, it might be inspired by a local event, for example, a celebration marking the rebuilding of London after the Great Fire of 1666, an object a child brings to school, a story or a poem the children have enjoyed, a piece of music, a visit to a museum or shipyard, a walk in the woods, a television programme or the first snow of winter.

Let us imagine that the theme has been taken from a topic drawn from the curriculum and demands that the children (our six-year-olds) follow a study of 'Where we live'. Such a theme could be treated quite narrowly or be inclusive of almost every area listed above. Areas which could be investigated by children as individuals, in small groups or by class might include:

- the village now
- the village long ago
- a village map
- shops
- places of work
- occupations of the inhabitants
- travel – road, rail, water and air
- new buildings, old buildings and ruined buildings
- the church
- materials used for building
- walks – the living countryside, lakes woods and streams

- leisure activities
- interviews with local people (or talks about what things we like in the past)
- our village within the county, landscape or nation.

This brief outline of a 'learning tree' or 'brain-map' provides ample opportunity to research, record, use words, make maps, paint and model, observe, comment, talk to adults and refer to books and other printed material. If the local church is old, or if there is a castle or manor house nearby, comparisons could be made of changing building styles and the materials used 'then' and 'now' and the idea of 'new', 'old' and 'very old'.

Within the possible areas of study listed above, are strands of mathematics, language, history, economics, culture, transport, natural science and art. Simple books, made by the children, could be used to collate and classify their discoveries; a museum table about the village could become the centre piece of a classroom display; walls could be decorated with photographs of past and present displayed alongside the children's own drawings and paintings. Observations spoken by the children could be written on card and mounted around the classroom to give unity to the presentation* and as a basis for the teaching of reading.

Almost any subject area can benefit from an holistic treatment of the kind described above. A study of the numbers one to nine could centre upon the children making a collection of the many places in which numbers are to be found – from street doors, to car plates and postage stamps. Where do we find numbers? How do we use them? What stories, poems, songs include numbers? What idioms employ numbers? I have expressed these questions in an adult form. Invite the children to think in a similar direction. The list of suggestions will be far more extensive.

Some themes emerge almost by accident. Andre brings a kite to school. Its arrival might trigger off a discussion on what shapes fly best and which shapes don't fly at all. In turn, this could take some children into a study of seed dispersal, butterflies, birds, Concorde or spacecraft.

**Always* use lower case lettering unless convention demands otherwise (eg capitals at the beginning of sentences and names). Most of the written language which children see around them is in lower case. Their growing appreciation of the 'pattern' or 'picture' of a word should not be confused by seeing it written in upper case within a school setting.

Each of these detailed examples indicate an open-ended approach to curriculum delivery. The skills of questioning, finding out, recording (at a level appropriate to the skills of the learner) are common to every subject area. Thus the curriculum is *process-driven* not product-led. It matters little *what* Eila or James learn when they are five, six or seven years old. It matters greatly *how* they are introduced to learning.

Integrating the curriculum (which a thematic approach demands) is about harmony, harmony in having, as a group, a shared interest, the harmony of a child with his personal stage of development, the harmony that comes from having children of *different* gifts, skills and knowledge prepared to share them with their fellows. Such an integrated approach is philosophically far removed from that which presents subjects within a tight academic corset. Segregation is the negation of harmony. It ignores the holistic way in which young children view their world.

When we achieve this ideal (which is as pertinent to the needs of adolescents as to those of six-year-olds) we will be nearer the dream expressed by the Italian educator and philosopher Pietro Prini. Speaking at a UNESCO conference in Paris in December 1989 he stated: 'We must seek to establish a curriculum for young people which has no subject barriers, a curriculum which is open but which is fed by a range of inputs – pedagogic, social, cultural.'

It is to a consideration of how such dreams might be realised that we shall now turn.

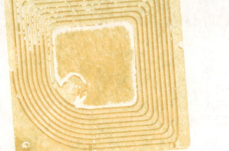

4 The classroom environment

Every child has been hot housed into an adult long before he has reached adulthood. A.S. NEILL (1883–1973)

We have established that the young learner comes to school with unique interests and a unique fund of knowledge. So whilst Alison or Tim may have been born on the same day, in the same year, in the same hospital ward, they enter school not as date stamped clones but as unique human beings. It follows that the classroom has to meet the needs of the individual and, *at the same time*, provide for each child to grow academically and emotionally.

Equipment

These twin demands create a healthy tension. Acceptance of individuality demands that the individuals who make up the group respect each other. Acceptance of individuality also means that the classroom has to be organised and equipped in such a way that a wide spectrum of needs can be met and satisfied. It follows that the provision of book and materials within the classroom must reflect the fact that in any class of six-year-olds (for example) there will be some who have barely reached the physical, intellectual, social and emotional level of a three-year-old. There will be others who have matured (in the areas listed above) so that we might consider them typically representative of children who are four, five or six. Living and learning alongside these children will be others who have an intellectual, social, physical and emotional maturity above their calendar years – functioning in a way more typical of a child of eight or nine. This is not to say that each child has a consistently even maturation level – the academically forward six-year-old might well be socially maladroit while his academically slower colleague possesses finely tuned motor skills. Thus the classroom space has to reflect the ever changing demands of the pupils who learn within it.

Let us assume that suitable furniture is available, for example, tables and chairs that can be grouped in a variety of ways, bookcases, cupboards for storage, tray units in which to keep small equipment and children's personal possessions and a number of larger tables on which collections and displays can be mounted (see Figure 5.1). Let us further assume that the teacher has a table and a chair and that there are also a couple of easy chairs that can be used as a focal point for informal class and group discussions. What other materials are needed to turn a furnished room into a learning base?

The list that follows is not exhaustive, but it does serve to indicate areas which need to be addressed.

Outdoor equipment

- A slide
- A climbing frame
- Trolleys and carts
- A swing
- Ride-on toys
- Bean bags
- Large balls
- Hoops
- Skittles

Classroom equipment

Sand-play equipment
- A free standing tray of sand (for example, 90cm × 60cm × 30cm)
- Tools for digging, scooping and shaping
- Buckets and containers for filling

Remember sand behaves differently when wet.

Water-play equipment
- A free standing water tray (for example, 90cm × 60cm × 30cm)
- Clean water (to approximately 20cm in depth)
- Assorted containers and pourers
- Funnels and tubes
- A sieve
- Bottles
- A sponge
- Things that float

- Things that sink
- Regular measures (for example, 250cc, 500cc or 1000cc jars and bottles)
- Toy boats

For ease of cleaning a small amount of liquid detergent should be added to the water.

Home-corner equipment
- A 'house' for play, suitably furnished with items such as a table, chairs, a sink, dolls and soft toys and a telephone.

Imaginative-play equipment
- Dressing up clothes
- Puppets and puppet theatre (these could be made by the children)
- Toy cars and road layouts
- Train set
- Doll's house and furniture
- Bricks (floor and table)
- Lego (or similar)

Creative equipment
- Paper of all kinds, sizes and colours, – kitchen paper, newspaper, sugar, foil, crepe, tissue, coloured sticky shapes, wallpaper and sweet papers
- Paint – pre-mixed colours are particularly suitable for this age group, finger paint and cold non-permanent water dyes
- Materials for collage and construction – fabric scraps, coloured netting, braid, felt, vilene, tape, wools and cottons, towelling, sequins and buttons
  Small boxes, toilet roll centres, packing straw, magazines, card, corrugated card, washed food containers (for example, margarine and butter packs and ice cream cartons)
- Natural materials – wood, seeds, shells, small stones, feathers, bark, twigs, raw wool and cane
  Soft modelling materials such as clay, synthetic clay like 'Plasticine'
- Drawing materials – wax crayons, pastels, chalk, coloured pencils, felt-tipped pens, charcoal, chalk and a fixative
- Tools – scissors, brushes in a range of sizes (2 to 16), plastic palette knives and mixing trays for paint

The teacher should also have a basic tool kit – saw, hammer, knife, screw driver, pliers, screws and nails
- Glues and fixatives – cold water paste, 'Alocryl' or similar PVA based adhesive and sticky tape

Table toys
- Constructional toys, such as standard Lego, jigsaw puzzles, dominoes, table bricks, 'Play people' and so on

Musical equipment
This equipment might be available within the room or stored centrally so that it could be shared with other classes.
- A range of percussion instruments (drums, triangles, tambourines, tambours, bells, tuned-wood blocks, xylophone and shakers) together with a variety of beaters
- Instruments made by the children (for example, shakers using dried peas in yoghurt pots and sandpaper blocks, 'pluckers' made by stretching thick elastic bands or violin gut tightly between two nails on a block of wood)

Mathematical equipment
The range is immense! Young children need equipment that will help them move from a world of 'concrete' things which they can touch, see and move in to the mathematical world of abstract ideas and processes and to encourage children in concept formation and to give them the confidence that is necessary to deal with abstractions such as weight, capacity, length, pattern, shape and the nature of number. (For example, what *is* special about oneness, fiveness, tenness; what do we mean by seven, and what sets sevenness apart from sixness or fiveness?). This mathematical equipment will include the following items.
- Items for counting such as beads, coloured bricks and cubes, coins, buttons and marbles
- Objects for sorting, such as any of the above plus small toys (for example farm animals), pebbles and shells and trays in which they can be stored
- Items for weighing. A simple balance which the children can use to experiment and deepen their understanding about weight and equality. The learning will be incidental but real and would initially come from the exploration of quite basic questions. How many large marbles exactly balance this cooking apple? If I change the apple for

a smaller one what happens? What can I use to 'weigh' ten feathers – would it be best to use dried peas, marbles or used postage stamps? At this early stage standard measures like gram and kilo need not be introduced. Understanding *why* standard measures become necessary follows upon and *should not precede* an appreciation of the nature and complexity of 'measuring' heaviness and lightness and of making comparisons between the weights of different objects.

- Equipment used for measuring. Once again a realisation of need for standard measures should be reached through experiment. Remember that lengths of string, rope and tape can be used for 'measuring' distance, just as effectively as expensive metre rods, 'click-wheels' and rulers. Children will also realise that time can be measured. Support material for their learning would include egg-timers, wooden and plastic clock faces with moveable hands, plastic and fabric digital clocks. Capacity can be explored through the equipment provided for water and sand play.
- Materials for developing number awareness. The counting and the sorting items listed above provide opportunity for children to count on (add), count back (subtract), and talk about numbers in a practical way. This experience can be extended through simple mathematical games like floor dominoes, the use of equalisers, number lines (that children can use for counting on from zero or for counting back from ten).
- Equipment for developing an appreciation of pattern. Underpinning much of mathematics is pattern and the way in which patterns reveal themselves. Regular geometric shapes such as the equilateral triangle can be fitted together to form other geometric shapes; rectangles, squares, circles, all have attributes that children can come to grasp through experiment followed by teacher-led discussion.

Library and language
- Books of all kinds – picture books which use few words, well illustrated information books, books of poetry and rhyme, story books. Remember that there will be some children in the class who are unable to read, some who have taken their first steps into reading (technically called 'reading ready') and some who are confident readers. The classroom book provision must reflect this fact – a wide range of books, readily accessible, will encourage book

use and inspire confidence. Books must be cared for, thoughtfully displayed throughout the classroom and stored in bookshelves which are child-friendly.
- Papers (white and coloured) and exercise books in which children can draw and write about their discoveries.
- Equipment that reflects contemporary technology – a tape recorder, slide projector, simple enlargers, a 35mm camera and a computer keyboard with display unit and a printer.

Despite the development of computer based technology (and the impact it has had on children's learning), books and the printed word continue to play a dominant and potent part in teaching and learning. It is obvious to adults why this should be so, but it is not always apparent to children that to employ modern technology effectively requires the user to be much more than computer-literate. In other words the significance of the printed word has been confined and enhanced by computer technology – rather than lessened.

Various strategies can be employed to help children grasp this point. Perhaps the most successful method is to introduce regular (termly) 'book weeks' into the school or class timetable.

A book week may take the form of a 'flood' – drenching the classroom(s) with printed materials of all kinds. In such a week the teacher would concentrate upon emphasising the value of books and the use of reading for information and for pleasure. The book-focus could be supported with displays in classrooms, corridors, the school entrance and the hall and extended to the public library to meet the librarian to find out about his or her work. It is also worth writing to publishers of children's books to discover if any of their authors live in the area. Most writers are happy to visit a school to meet their readers.

In one school where I taught, a member of staff arranged a 'Book Bang'. On a particular day during a book week, teachers, parents and children dressed as their favourite character from literature. The conventional school programme was suspended and replaced with story telling, poems, plays and dramatic presentations. There were book sales, book-making exhibitions, and displays about particular authors and their work. Throughout the day, parents played a full part, sometimes as storytellers to a group, sometimes by reading to an individual child. One parent entertained an audience of adults and children with a 25 minute presentation of Stanley Holloway monologues – including 'Albert and the Lion'. Her Lancashire accent,

The classroom environment

Figure 4.1 The classroom where the walls tell of the learning which has taken place

of which she remained justly proud, was a joy to hear!

Flexible space in the classroom

Extensive though this list of equipment appears, the organiser of a child-centred classroom will also need to create spaces which allow for flexible use.

Interest areas

For example, an interest area like an attractive wall display linked to what topic is currently being studied could be created in one section of the classroom. If 'things made of glass' is the current interest and the wall display reflects this then the 'interest area' also can become a museum. A table carrying bottles and containers and glass objects of all kinds (as well as books about glass) can be, for example, placed close to the wall display.

Such a display does not remain static. Examples on the table are regularly changed; fresh objects and books are added to reflect the children's deepening interests. Similarly the children's paintings and drawings of glass objects can be added to the wall display together with their spoken observations (recorded by the teacher and included as a wall commentary): Mary said, 'Looking through green glass makes the world one colour'.

Interest areas can be created around almost any topic. For example scientific thinking could be triggered through a table of simple electrical experiments based upon a dry battery, circuit board, bulb and switch; an appreciation of how plants respond to light and water through growing things – seeds, spring flowers, onions, carrots, potatoes. The interest area might be used to explore colour – displaying things that are yellow for one week, things that are blue next – it might focus upon objects from other lands, toys, or things we found on the shore – in the woods – on a walk. An exhibition might begin with a single object (an old alarm clock, for example) and grow into a collection of objects that have numbers on them, of things made of metal, of objects which make a noise or that have parts which move.

Interest areas allow children to become participators and contributors. Such areas need to be kept alive, with exhibits and themes regularly changed. A dead, dusty display in a classroom is a

The classroom environment

Figure 4.2 *A classroom must provide space for individual needs to be met*

Starting school: the vital years

powerful indicator of a teacher with a dying, dusty mind!

Classroom layout

We have the equipment. We have the materials. We must next consider their spread across the room. It is difficult to describe on the printed page how best to physically arrange a classroom. Every room is different in shape, size and position within the school building. The following generalisations may, however, be helpful.

- Organise the classroom space by activity. Try to determine where best to place the 'wet' and 'dry' activities (such as clay modelling,

Figure 4.3 Classroom layout must allow for individual interests to be satisfied

sand and water tray, painting: reading writing, constructional toys). Obviously 'wet' activities need to be set near a sink or water supply *and* away from the classroom door. The wet area will be one where considerable activity occurs; areas for quiet activities may well have a more blurred focus, for they can be used for both mathematics and language. Thus they should be located close to the mathematical apparatus and the book corner which contains the classroom library.
- Create a multi-purpose area. This space can be principally used for table top activities – writing, drawing, playing with small toys.
- Set up a home corner/play corner. This can easily be tucked into a corner of the room and take up a minimum of space. This gives a degree of privacy to the children who are playing within it.
- Identify areas suitable for displays and interest tables. This might be determined by the position of pin boarding and furniture that is fixed to the wall. (In some schools display areas are limited. 'Built-in' display areas can also be very restrictive on the arrangement of the classroom.)
- Create a space where children can gather together for stories, poetry, discussion, and so on. Small children take up very little space when sitting on the floor.
- Make sure there is enough circulation space. Having organised the furniture and set out the materials, make sure that you and the children can move within the classroom and between the furniture without difficulty.
- Make sure that the materials and equipment that the children need to use are readily available and are all within easy reach.

A room laid out in this way, is divided by function. The children, who are based within it, are undertaking a range of different but mutually compatible activities. This way of using the classroom is similar to the way in which we use a house or a flat. We define space by how we use it. We *could* sleep in the kitchen but we don't. Instead we keep the tools there that are needed for the preparation of food. Appropriateness determines how we use space and this is how it should be within the space we call a classroom.

Teaching implies an intention to follow a particular set of activities and processes in order to reach a specific and clearly defined goal (for example, to have Tina leave your class able to read a simple text, add and subtract numbers up to 30, become socially responsible and caring...). We must ensure that our intentions do not remain vague dreams but are realised.

5 Some days in school

We need to teach our children how to learn.   PRINCE KROPTKIN,
Russian Revolutionary, 1917

It is impossible to create the atmosphere of a classroom on the printed page. When the relationship between teacher and taught is positive, the feeling in the room can be described as magical; when the relationship is tense, the feeling can be described as jagged and destructive. To avoid the luxury of using either extreme (romanticism or cynicism) I will attempt to be clinical in my description of the processes of teaching and of learning within a space we call a classroom. To this end, the following description relates to the classroom shown in Figure 5.1, which is an actual classroom organised by the teacher, Jenny, who planned it and taught six-year-olds within it.

Arranging the classroom

The first thing to notice is that each part of the classroom has a particular focus. To the left of the door is an area that is both *home-base* and book corner. Here in the home-base children gather, when necessary, throughout the day. The teacher's (easy) chair backs against her worktable. This area, formed from the part of the room that is covered with carpet, is sufficiently large for the class of 28 children to sit comfortably on the floor at her feet. This home-base is clearly defined with furniture – a tray unit (with open, plastic trays in which children keep their personal belongings), a storage and display unit and a book trolley form a rectangle (the two walls providing its third and fourth sides). When children gather around their teacher, this rectangular frame encourages shared togetherness, reduces the distance between teacher and taught and prevents children from becoming distracted by movement and activity in other parts of the classroom (or in the playground outside the window).

To the right of the door is a block of tables. These have been placed

Starting school: the vital years

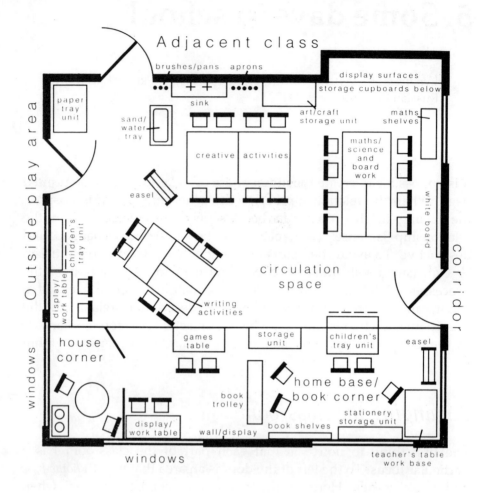

Figure 5.1 A classroom plan

close to the white marker board. Nearby are storage cupboards and shelves containing *mathematical apparatus,* arranged in such a way as to give easy access to the children.

Beyond this mathematical area is a space given over to *practical activities* – painting, picture making, clay work, modelling. The sand or water tray is near the sink, as are the brushes and pans which will be used throughout the day to keep the floor clean.

Occupying the centre of the room is a block of tables which are used for *clean activities* such as *writing*, book making, table games. In the far corner of the room are two doors, one opening on to an outside play area, the other into a neighbouring classroom.

The fourth corner of the classroom consists of a *house/dramatic play* area in which children can dress up and involve themselves in games of make-believe.

Looking around the room individual tables provide additional space on which to put out equipment and to mount displays relating to on-going studies. Beyond the book corner/home-base, for example, is a wall display about things made with glass. The table beneath it contains a small exhibition of bottles, bowls, marbles and coloured ornaments.

It is noticeable that small equipment – pencils, scissors and paint brushes – is stored in pots and trays, each clearly labelled. The pencils, lead and coloured, are sharp; the brushes are clean; the paint is pre-mixed and ready for use; books stand in almost every available space, their covers showing, inviting children to take them down and look at them.

So much for the room, a room which even without children in it comments upon the way the teacher sees his or her role and purpose. Having structured the space, how is it used by the children who are to learn within it?

Classroom use

Let us turn to a typical day, a day which is a little way into the school year. The children have come to know Jenny and Jenny has come to know each of them as unique individuals with strengths and weaknesses, gifts and interests. (She has come to know something of their homes too, of their parents and their anxieties and hopes.) The children arrive informally in the classroom and collect in the home-base. Sitting around Jenny's chair they talk quietly to each other, describing the events of the previous evening, the programmes they watched on television, things seen on the way to school. It is Mark's birthday and he has brought a letter to school from his uncle who lives in Spain. Jenny sees this as an opportunity to mention Mark's birthday, to talk about the postage stamps (this one seems to record a famous happening), and about Spain (Has anyone been there? How do you get to Spain from the United Kingdom? Where is Spain on the globe?) Talk encourages children to put their ideas and personal knowledge into words. Jenny regards this 'giving space for talk' as a very important part of her work as a teacher of young children. The informal incidental discussion,

Starting school: the vital years

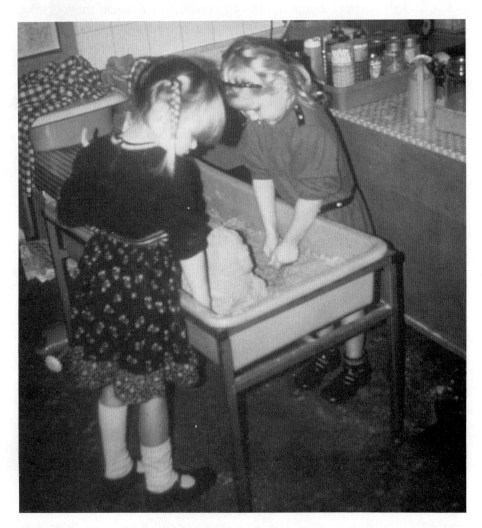

Figure 5.2 Play, a vital part of the learning process

triggered off by Mark's birthday and a postage stamp, lasts for some ten minutes. There is a pause, a change in emphasis and direction.

'Yesterday, before we went home we made plans for this morning. Let me remind you. Those who were going to paint a picture about the Road Safety puppets that came yesterday, can go to the painting table and begin. Remember to put on an apron and cover the table with newspaper before you start.'

Eight of the 28 children leave the group.

'Writers?' Six children take a large drawing book from a pile on the shelf beside Jenny. In these books children draw and colour a picture. Under the picture they write an appropriate sentence. Some children need much help from Jenny, others very little. Taking lead and coloured pencils from a tray, the six children troop over to the writing table, chat for a moment amongst themselves and settle down to draw and write.

Jenny nods to four more children who seem to know that they can begin the day in the play house. Three others take out a large box of Lego, some 'Play people' and a tray of small coloured bricks. They find a space on the carpet on the other side of the book trolley and begin to build a castle. The remaining seven children follow Jenny to the mathematics table, are given some coloured plastic and cubes and begin to use them to explore ways of making the number ten – one red cube linked to nine yellow cubes; five blue cubes to five pink cubes; three red cubes linked to four green cubes and three white cubes ....

The cubes are arranged and rearranged. There is much talk. Some recording of numbers takes place but Jenny seems more concerned that their talk really clarifies their understanding of the nature of number.

Jenny periodically leaves the mathematics group to help children on the writing table, to admire the slowly growing castle, to quieten the excitement of the two children who are re-enacting a particularly noisy quarrel they had obviously observed at home. One boy has finished his painting. He brings it to Jenny for comment. She admires it and suggests that he leaves it to dry but 'finds something else to do'. He washes his hands, goes to the book corner and begins to read. (He seems to be reading fluently. Certainly the size of the type size would be appropriate for a child of nine or ten.)

The activities last for about 45 minutes. Time for a change of activity?

Jenny gives the whole class a reminder that soon things will change. 'In five minutes we will begin to clear up.' She turns for a moment to the castle builders. 'It's such a marvellous castle I think you should leave it for us to look at. You could tell us about the different parts you've made and why you've built it as you have.'

The notice of intention to stop is important. Like us, children need to be given time to prepare to change an activity. The activities seem to wind down naturally. Books are returned to shelves, equipment put away. The paintings are left to dry and the class gather again in the home-base.

The weather happens to be fine and Jenny feels that a change of activity is appropriate. A quiet word and the whole class (except Peter who is cleaning brushes and wiping the painting table dry) go to the outside play area to skip with ropes and hoops, use large balls to improve their catching skills and plastic hockey sticks to hit soft balls around the play space.

This brief physical activity is followed by something much quieter. The children put away the ropes, sticks and balls and gather on the carpet in a circle around James and Mandy – who spend some minutes telling a story about a king who lives in the red castle and who has certain problems with his three daughters, his six sons and an angry dragon. Jenny then takes over. Once more sitting at her feet in the home-base they listen to some poetry and a folk song on tape. The children join in both. The poems seem to have been selected because the children are familiar with them, the folk song because they know the tune and the chorus. (Whilst this is happening Mandy and James are dismantling the castle. They do it quietly, joining in the singing and recitation as they do so.)

The remainder of the morning is similar to that described above. The early morning mathematicians paint and draw; Jenny has a group by the white marker board who are practising letter formation and handwriting; a third group are playing matching games with dominoes and picture cards; four children are doing jigsaws.

It is clear that Jenny has a plan for her day and a clear idea of the activities which the children are to undertake. She moves from her writing group to help and advise other children as and when they need her. Her interventions are considered and deliberate, encouraging acceptable behaviour in a quiet, friendly voice rather than commenting upon error.

Again activities are allowed to draw to a natural, gentle end. There are no bells in this school that shape the day, no tight timetables of specific activities for this class.

The home-base again. Discussion about the afternoon's work is followed by a story (a favourite of Mark's, to celebrate his birthday). The story from a large picture book is presented quite slowly, the pictures being shown to the children as the story unfolds for their comments and enjoyment.

Lunch over, the afternoon begins in the home-base. A new topic is being introduced – 'Floating and Sinking'.

'What do we mean by float?' asks Jenny, pointing to a glass bowl containing water which stands on the table behind her. The question leads to much discussion. A pencil is put in the bowl, then a drawing pin, an eraser, a coin and a piece of thin card. 'So why do some things

Some days in school

Figure 5.3 Problem-solving through technology

float and some things sink?' The silence which followed this question is followed by a period of sustained but gentle questioning as Jenny teases out the children's ideas.

During lunch-time Jenny has filled three large plastic trays with water and has placed them on the wet 'activity' table. Around each bowl is a range of different objects – plastic boats, a paper clip, a match box, a large nail, some bottles, a toy car, a building brick, some paper and some scraps of cooking foil. 'Could we make a test', asks Jenny, 'to see if we can find out why some things float and some things sink? Is there any way you could help an object that sinks to float?'

It would have been impossible for all the children to experiment at the same time. To make the organisation easier, Jenny has divided the class into groups that were known to the children. She has given a colour of each group. Red group are to be the 'scientists' this afternoon and they go to the floating/sinking table to begin their experiments. The children in green and blue groups have 'choosing time' when they can undertake an activity of their own choice. For yellow group there is writing to complete (obviously it is not made up of children who had worked in books in the morning). The remaining children read individually to Jenny, their progress recorded in her personal 'record book of children's progress'.

The day draws towards its close. The children help pack away equipment and tidy the room. Once again the whole class gathers in the home-base. This is a time of coming together, quiet talk and sharing. The children who have experimented with water describe what they have discovered – 'You can make a nail float on a piece of paper', says Tom, 'but not a small piece.' 'But the nail *did* sink', says Mary, 'when the paper got too wet.' Jenny listens, comments, talks about the paintings that have been done that day, praises Peter for a page in his writing/picture book and invites Jane to read the poem she has found about birthdays (Jane needs her confidence boosting. This is a way of doing it).

Before the final story which will end the day, Jenny speaks about how the day will begin tomorrow. She describes the activities that will be on offer, which group will begin with the water experiment, who will write.

While identifying the clear commitment of some children to specific activities, Jenny gave an opportunity to others to choose between a range of options. Each child *knew* that Jenny expected 'work' of them. Each understood that 'work' centred upon mathematics, language and certain clearly defined studies. Each *knew* that their experiments in floating and sinking would require some form of recording in pictures and words, that using cubes to find out about the number ten would involve them in eventually writing down their findings.

A number of significant strands can be drawn from this description of a class of six-year-olds at work.

1 The importance of creating a room that is flexible but gives a clear structure to the range of activities being undertaken. In the school where I was headteacher, every member of the school staff spent the day before the beginning of each school term for classroom preparation. A teacher once remarked to me: 'One day spent quietly in school, without children, to plan the classroom space and the materials within it is so worthwhile. I'm able to resolve problems before they arise. It makes teaching so much easier.'

2 The importance of having material and equipment available *when it is needed*. In the classroom described above, Jenny spent a few

moments at the end of the day making sure that pencils were sharp, that paste pots had paste in them, that small equipment was complete and tidy.

3 The importance of keeping records of
   (a) group activities,
   (b) individual progress, for example, in reading.
(This aspect of the teacher's work is outlined in the pages which follow.)

4 The importance of talk as a means of developing and evaluating children's understanding and the importance of giving time to *listening*.

5 The importance of having a vision, of setting goals that children can achieve as individuals, within a group, and as a class. In the day described above, Jenny did not simply wait for children to ask questions about floating and sinking. She created a situation that drew upon the children's natural curiosity and the knowledge that they already possessed (such as the embedded knowledge that some things float and some things sink). Her teaching programme was based upon a defined curriculum area. She presented it in a form which demanded that the children be active in their response – not just passive onlookers.

6 The importance of responding to the immediacy of children's interests – even if it is only a stamp on a birthday card.

7 The importance of giving praise and honest comment. Children quickly 'read' the insincere observation. Children like to be praised when they have really given of their best. Praise lavished on work of poor quality debases praise given for work that is outstanding.

The school day described above provides a core on which to build. Of course not all days will be identical. Some days may see the class in a museum, visiting a farm or exploring the local countryside or town. The school day following such an experience may be devoted entirely to drawing, painting, modelling, mapping and writing about it. Provided a reasonable balance of subject areas is achieved over a month, it does not matter if, for example, formal mathematics is missed for a day, or the folk dance session is held over until the following week.

A perceptive teacher (like Jenny) creates a framework to ensure that the children have a range of opportunities – to explore mathematics, science, language and cultural and social studies. *These opportunities will be planned and delivered against her children's present*, not against a curriculum plan drawn up many months earlier.

It is the interaction of teacher and child within a carefully structured learning environment that I have sought to describe above. It is clear that much depended upon Jenny and the strategies she adopted.

A History project

Six months have passed. Let us once again return to the same classroom and examine a topic which stems directly from an area of the National Curriculum.

The History Curriculum clearly identifies the skills and concepts which are central to the learning of history and the attainment levels which might be expected of a child in the early years of schooling.

As a whole-class activity the children in Jenny's class have been engaged in a project entitled 'All about me'. Jenny hopes that such a study will allow her to establish the fact that history is about people and that each person (even each child in her class) has a history.

The layout and appearance of Jenny's classroom has not radically changed because a new topic is under way. Maths apparatus continues to dominate one corner of the room, and the displays around it show that the children are concerned with a study of body measures. (Table tops have been measured in hand spans, the width of the room and the height of the doorways in human feet, a reading book in thumbs. Questions supporting the display invite children – and their parents – to wonder why Hank needed fewer handspans to measure the desk than did Salem and how Nina managed to measure the door in feet without walking up the wall.)

The importance which Jenny places upon language work is also apparent. A quick glance at the children's writing and painting suggests that 'When I grow up I would like to be ...' has provided opportunity for a wide range of imaginative writing. 'When I grow up', writes six-year-old James, 'I want to play for Arsenal or be a brain surgeon.' Wendy 'wants to be like my mum' and Tipy 'hopes to be a pilot so I can go to see my grandmother in Bangladesh.' Some of this writing is in simple print, some in joined script. One piece has been printed on the class computer.

One large area of wall is given over to a display entitled 'When I was young ...', at first sight an odd title for a group of children who had yet to reach the age of seven. Along this wall, at child's eye level, runs a time line. It is quite short, covering no more than 60 years. On one part of the line, around the years 1986 and 1987 much information has been gathered. Peter's declaration 'I was born on October 23rd.' This is typical of the statements which cluster round these years. Further back along the line children have written similar statements about the birthdays of their brothers and sisters – and of the adults in their lives.

On a table near the time-line and on the wall above it are photographs of the children when they were babies, of their parents and of 'events' of the past which they remember. There is also a large collection of objects which have associations with the past. Everything is clearly labelled. 'I had these boots when I was a baby,' writes Paula. 'This is my favourite toy bear,' writes Fred. There is also a display of children's booklets in which they have made collections of their early memories.

Morning break is over. Jenny gathers the children round her. She introduces them to the visitor they have been expecting, Mrs Ethel Brickton who lives in a road near to the school. The introduction is gentle and very informal.

'This is Mrs Brickton. She has lived in Nightingale Street all her life. She is going to tell you what it was like when she was a small child ....'

Ethel Brickton, a lady in her late sixties is a natural communicator. She tells the children of her early memories of school, of the games she played in the playground ('Hopscotch' and 'He'), of things she did not have – a record player, a transistor, a television. She tells of 'going hopping' (hop picking) in September and October, of a holiday (just one day!) in Southend, of going 'down the Lane' on Sundays with her father (the Lane was a Sunday market). She tells of watching 'her old school come down and a new one go up'. When she has finished questions tumbled out.

'What did you do if you didn't have a telly?'
'Is your house still old fashioned? Do you have a washing machine now?'
'Do you still have gas light?'

The session over, the children write about their visitor as a *whole-class* activity. Jenny writes difficult spellings on the white board (which many members of the class also transfer into their personal dictionaries). The pieces of writing are then illustrated with pictures of Mrs Brickton – a real person who has shared her past with them.

After lunch the children gather once more around Jenny's chair in the home-corner. They have had a little time to reflect on Mrs Brickton's visit. While the memory of it was still vivid, Jenny raises questions central to the study of history. 'How was Nightingale Street different when Mrs Brickton was a child? How was it the same? What games did she play? What games do you play now? What work did she do? Do you know anybody that does this work (a biscuit packer) today?' The children do not know that Jenny is exploring the historical concept of 'continuity and change', but her aim is clear to them, showing that, through people, past and present become one.

Mrs Brickton has shown the children a picture of her house in a war time newspaper cutting. Jenny asks whether things like photographs and things like old toys and old books help give an idea of what it was like 'long ago'. The idea of historical evidence and the value of oral history is not developed by Jenny. She is simply sowing an idea which can be developed at some later stage.

Let us reflect once again on this brief classroom visit. The spoken word, the printed word, the opportunity to listen, understand and comment, the ability to cope with ideas like 'now' and 'then', 'time past and time present' are all elements in the development of historical thinking.

Yet this topic pulled in far more than history. Jenny used an area of the National Curriculum to unite language, mathematics (body measurements), place (where I was born) and time. Each of these sub-topics tied into other National Curriculum 'targets'. What Jenny was doing was to present learning in a meaningful way and meeting curriculum goals without allowing her children to become disenchanted at the process. In this way the curriculum would not constrict but liberate.

Jenny, a sensitive and creative teacher, determined quite deliberately to build upon the level of understanding that each of her children had reached, to construct a theme to which individual children could contribute something of themselves. The building of a personal history, backed up with photographs and personal artefacts, was an active, on-going process. In exploring his or her own past each child learned something of *how* to learn (in psychological terms 'constructed their own system of meaning'). In developing these ideas, they engaged their minds as well as their hands, using language, written and spoken, to express their thoughts and ideas.

'How did you do washing without a machine?' is not just a question about cleanliness. Implicit is also the thought 'Mrs Brickton lived in a time before I was born. This time was not the same as now.' Perhaps for some children the thought extended still further – 'and now is not going to be the same as tomorrow' (which the activity 'When I grow up' seemed to confirm).

One other aspect of the way in which Jenny handled this topic is worthy of mention. Jenny's understanding of how young children learn caused her to avoid abstractions. The whole topic was contextualised by and flowed from the children's first-hand experience, that of being an individual, alive *now* in the 1990s. Mrs Brickton was not an abstraction. She was alive, touchable, meetable on human terms. The children were able to grasp the link between her physical presence in their classroom and their own studies. For learning to be successful, the young learners must understand why they are doing a particular task.

Some months later when Mrs Brickton's visit had become little more than a distant memory and the group were quietly engaged in a study of 'growing things', Robert brought a flat iron into school to be sold at a bring and buy sale. 'Do you think Mrs Brickton had one of these?' he asked Jenny.

Jenny used the question to lead the class back to the topic on which they had devoted so much time in the spring term. The informal discussion revived memories, and prompted moments of insight which (Jenny said) had not been obvious before. As Rosie (not the most articulate six-year-old observed), 'They could have had no electric in them days – could they then?'

This description of one 'piece of learning' within a National Curriculum framework leads me to make a final point. In constructing learning programmes, we should realise that we can never complete a topic in such a way that it may henceforth be ignored.

Young children build on where they are and bring fresh thoughts to the knowledge they already possess. J.S. Bruner's paradigm (which presents learning and understanding in the form of a spiral in which past knowledge and experience gives shape to new ideas) provides a useful framework for the teacher of young children.

It is this awareness which makes working with young children such a rewarding – and challenging – task.

All about me
A summary of links between National Curriculum subject areas

History	Activities
Knowledge of historical context in programmes of study	Sequencing Identifying differences and similarities between past and present Describing change Recognising that some things change and others stay the same
Interpretation	Recognising the difference between a fairytale and a story about past times
Use of historical sources	Mrs Brickton – oral history The use of artefacts

Science (links)	Activities
Exploration and observation of materials and events in their immediate environment	Discussing personal growth, materials and fabrics used in baby clothes
Analysis of processes of life, including energy	Making a personal account of their own day – and the changes in their days as they grow older Investigating food, exercise, rest Medicine, changes over time Finding out about food today – and when Mrs Brickton was young

English (links)	Activities
Awareness of the importance of speaking and listening and the ability to express oneself effectively through a variety of speaking and listening activities	Participating as listeners and speakers in all aspects of the topic Listening attentively Responding to instructions Describing an event
Development of the ability to read and to respond to all types of writing	Using books and dictionaries Listening and responding to stories Expressing opinions Reading material related to the topic
Construction and communication of meaning through writing	Retelling a story (When I was 3 ...) Sequencing events Producing a piece of independent writing Producing a piece of non-chronological writing (a description of Mrs Brickton)

Geography (links)	Activities
Sense of place	Observing and talking about local areas Using a street map Making themselves familiar with local landmarks Describing journeys to local places

Mathematics (links)	Activities
Use of numbers for practical tasks	Recording such things as birthdays, house numbers Writing and graphing their findings (body measurements)
Notation	Sequencing Producing a time-line Ordering by size and weight (body measurements)

Recording and handling data	Recording information about themselves
Music (links)	*Activities*
Listening	Listening to songs and game chants which children sang and recited when Mrs Brickton was at school
Art (links)	*Activities*
The development of visual perception	Portraits: 'Me'. 'Me and my family', 'Mrs Brickton' Family photographs
The development of visual literacy	Using a variety of wet and dry media for picture making related to the theme (paint, pastel, chalk, pencil, felt pen)

In this brief table* I have consciously avoided tying the specific elements of consecutive Key Stages (1 and 2) to particular levels of attainment. The purpose of my summary is to indicate a process rather than to suggest that Jenny began with and linked her activities to an inflexible structure based upon external 'targets' and 'levels'. If the National Curriculum is to be delivered effectively each teacher *must* relate the broad sweep of its content to the children in his or her care. Curriculum targets (like the National Curriculum itself) are rarely static. In every country in which I have taught, the national curriculum has been seen as an ever-changing element of educational provision. Sometimes the curriculum has been changed because it has proved politically expedient to do so, sometimes because the plans made by its designers are undeliverable in the classroom. A brief review of the changes made in the curriculum documents in England since 1989, indicates that England's educational planners have been – in this respect – no more successful than their colleagues on the European mainland.

---

* For ease of reference, 'spreads' of information can be summarised on proforma. Some examples are included in the Appendix.

6 The creative dimension

We still concentrate on facts rather than values, on memory rather than understanding, on what can be measured to the neglect of what cannot.   ALEC CLEGG, 1969

In the preceding chapter we looked, at some length, at the work of a gifted and creative teacher. Central to all that I have written so far is the firm belief that children are creative too. It follows, therefore, that if learning and teaching are to be effective, creativity (which is possessed in some measure by all human beings) must be fostered in the classroom.

When a young child picks up a crayon and scribbles on a paper a representation of 'my mum' or turns an empty cornflakes packet into an imaginary car he or she is conveying something of a universal need to create, make and build. As Herbert Read stressed in *Education through Art* (1943), the drive to create has provided the key to human development, enabling men and women to shape their environment. We have only to consider the sophistications of modern living (credit cards, central heating, and the motor car) to appreciate the strength of Read's thesis.

More recently, Arthur Ash, the American tennis star, emphasised the importance of the creative dimension in his posthumously published book *Days of Grace*. Writing to his daughter (knowing he was dying of Aids) he observed: 'I have always been moved by art and poetry. Don't let anyone tell you that either one is frivolous or expendable or inferior to making money. Without either or music, life would be dry and without feeling. Art comes from an urge as primal as that of survival itself.'

The value of the arts in developing and sustaining the human being so movingly expressed by Ash has been endorsed by many other writers. Peter Brinson in a trenchant article 'Arm against the Philistines' in the *Times Educational Supplement*, of 17 September 1993, suggests that curiosity is the force which powers learning, a force we ignore at our peril. 'Curiosity', he says, 'is the motor of education, curiosity shared by teachers and learners in so many different ways.'

Encouraging creativity

But before we attempt to examine how best to ensure that young children's enthusiasm for the arts is allowed to flower, it is necessary to define creativity. S. Field, sometime lecturer at the London Institute of Education, provided his students with a clear and simple definition: 'to invent with spontaneity and inspiration'. It seems to me that this phrase provides a focus for all teachers of young children. It conveys the exhilaration with which the five, six and seven-year-old expresses a personal view of the world through pictures, models, sounds, movement and words. Implicit in the definition is that the young creator possesses a free ranging imagination as well as a mind capable of presenting unexpected images.

Watch a nursery child put on a pair of high-heeled shoes and a Sloane Ranger hat and toss a giant sized handbag over her shoulder. Listen to the language. Admire the walk. Then, take time to reflect upon the interpretation of her world through *her* eyes, marvelling that one so young is able to 'read', so meticulously, the adults who people her world.

At a subsequent stage in the child's development ideas spoken and mimed will become ideas written, taped or recorded on video. Would any adult dare to begin the Christmas story as six-year-old Alec did? 'Mary', he wrote, 'was a woman who had a firm belief in angels ....'

When children are encouraged not to be afraid of expressing themselves in their creative work they respond totally, immersing themselves in the process. Such immersion involves the discovery about the way materials behave and the different forms in which ideas can be presented. More significantly it involves learning.

Caldwell Cook, (see page 19) argued in *The Playway* (1946) that by building a classroom/school environment which was sympathetic to young children's innate desire to 'make and do', learning would be enhanced. 'The final appreciation in life and in study is to put oneself into the things studied, to entirely live there.'

Such beliefs and attitudes jar unhappily with many of the proclaimed educational aims of the past decade.

In the 1980s and 1990s, many children have grown up in a society which seems indifferent to aesthetic values; in a climate which seems to be marked by an insensitivity to human needs. The social problems which stem from a decaying social infrastructure and the increasing isolation which this brings to the poor, the weak and the vulnerable,

The creative dimension

Figure 6.1 The creative dimension – making a theatre

Starting school: the vital years

Figure 6.2 Recording a visit

together with high levels of unemployment and homelessness have occurred at a time when teachers have been pressurised 'to return to basics'.

Yet, as H.G. Wells observed through the voice of Mr Polly, in *The History of Mr Polly* (1910), a school programme which treats the young as though they were university academics is bound to fail. How dare we, asks Mr Polly, so obstruct the curiosities and willingness of children that their world becomes 'no longer a wonderland of experience but simply geography and history'? To which I would add this. At a time when the economic and social climate outside the classroom is far from secure, it becomes even more important for the school to be a place where creativity is allowed to flower.

Readers of this book who are parents, or who have watched young children develop, know that they do indeed 'live in a wonderland of experience' or, as John Dewey put it, live in 'a world of persons and personal interests rather than a realm of facts and laws'.

Perhaps it is because young children are possessed of such a deep sense of wonder that they are a joy to teach. It is a willingness by the adults in their lives to share children's wonder through words written and spoken, through pictures and models, though music and drama that brings to the early years in school qualities of integrity and honesty that tend to become less obvious in the later years of childhood.

The apparent clash of curriculum demands with children's needs to be creative should not disturb the thoughtful teacher. The creative classroom will also tend to be the effective one, the one in which children learn. By giving space in the daily programme for children to talk before they write and space to think before they paint, construct, draw or use the computer, we also give each child an opportunity to bring something of themselves into the process. A creative environment is not one in which a class of six-year-olds produce 30 identical Christmas calendars, 30 identical Easter bunnies or 30 identical Mother's Day cards. A creative environment is one in which children are empowered to present their own thoughts and ideas in their own way.

Robin Tanner, an educator and artist, argued that acceptance by teachers of the child's 'way of looking' was an integral part of a creative environment, a classroom where children are encouraged to 'think and act for themselves, to call upon their own interests and resources. Too often they are not given enough to work upon or the work they are called to do is desultory.'

Figure 6.3 Playing a part

The check list Key questions, which is included on page 72, implies that individual creativity should not be measured against a common mark or standard. 'Measurement' or 'success' is much more than judging a child's poem, piece of writing or painting by the 'worth' of the end product – the impact it makes upon the reader or the viewer. Of course the final piece of work is important. Equally

The creative dimension

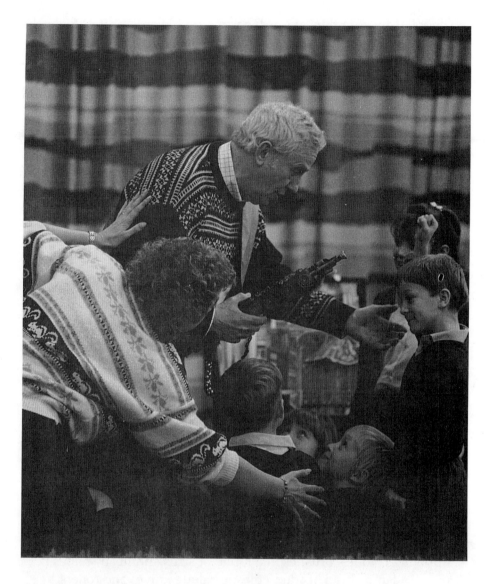

Figure 6.4 Working with a professional artist. John Dobson of the Royal Opera explores music and drama with six-year-olds

important, however, is the struggle which each child undertook to achieve the particular end.

Young children's appreciation of the nature of the creative process can be helped in all manner of ways. Many local and national arts organisations are happy to support schools in this area, perhaps by funding craftsmen and women so that they can spend time as 'artists in school'. Museum education departments have dedicated, over the past 15 years, ever more of their limited resources to ensure that visits to exhibitions by young children are made as meaningful as possible. Indeed a 'hands-on' approach to learning is as common in most museums today as was the silent 'eyes-on' approach of my own childhood. Exposure to the arts by visits to special concerts and theatre performances are also an important part of the creative programme I am attempting to describe.

Such experiences help the young learner understand that society includes adults who also celebrate making, doing and creating. In a way this human dimension establishes a dialogue between the young person as consumer of a cultural past, the young person as an apprentice living alongside adults who are creating a cultural present and who, in turn, provide inspiration and direction to the child as contributor to the quality of the environment within school and of the society beyond its walls.

Such external resources as we draw upon (whether they be the enthusiasm of a local weaver or the education department of an international dance company) need to be continually reinforced within the classroom. In order to make sure that the classroom is adequately resourced, periodic checks are advisable in the areas listed below.

Resources

Materials
Is there a wide range of materials for the following activities?
- Colouring – powder paint/pre-mixed tempera colour, cold water dyes, inks, chalks, pastels, oil crayons, oil pastels, wax crayons, felt-tipped pens, coloured pencils, drawing pencils (3B through F and HB to 3H) and charcoal
- Applying colour – brushes in a range of sizes and head shapes (2 to 16, round and chisel headed), plastic palette knives and rollers
- Glueing and sticking – cold water paste, glue sticks/pencils, PVA adhesive (such as 'Alocryl', 'Marvin') and sticky tape
- Constructing – waste material of all kinds (toilet roll centres, card and wood off cuts, fabric scraps), boxes, ribbons, braids, buttons, beads and corrugated packing card
- Joining – glues (see above), string, wire, cottons, wools and threads, nails, screws, paper clips and fasteners
- Support – sugar and construction paper in a wide range of colours,

newsprint, cartridge, scraps of hard-board, corrugated card, metallic paper, crepe and tissue

Tools
What tools are readily available for the following.
- The children – scissors (which cut), saw and board, metal rule, light hammer, screw driver, pliers, stapler and staples (paper), crewel and darning needles and aprons
- The teacher – good quality scissors, guillotine (or paper cutter), set of tools for working in wood, sharp safety knife, hand drill, decoration brushes, stapler and staples (wall) and safety ruler
- Creative play – how well is the classroom stocked with constructional toys (bricks, Lego, *large size* Meccano), dressing up clothes, hats, puppets, tuned percussion instruments and 'home-corner' furniture?
- Storage – how are the materials/equipment stored and made available to the children? Are creative materials locked away or easily accessible? Are individual children given responsibility for keeping specific items clean (for example paint brushes, junk box and dressing-up clothes)? Would it be possible or worthwhile to invest in drawer units or paper bins?

Time

Is sufficient time given to creative work – spoken and written language, making and doing, dance, movement, drama? How can I achieve a better balance in the daily/weekly programme, taking into account the restraints of the school in which I work (for example, timetable of school hall, outside play space, weather)?

Presentation

How do I receive the children's work? Do I need to find more time to talk with the children about their creations (be the creation a painting, a poem, or a castle imaginatively built of wooden bricks)? How well do I present the children's paintings, writing, their mathematical discoveries? Could I improve the presentation by mounting it before displaying it – or by encouraging children to border and decorate their written work?

Delivery

When I present new ideas do I encourage an open ended response – or does my method of presentation restrain and shape it? How well do I adapt my demands in the light of children's ideas?

Expectation

Do I expect enough of my children in areas of creative work? Are my demands too low?

Key questions on creativity

When young children are involved in creative activities are they:
- given sufficient time to look and observe
- given opportunity to talk about the work they are about to begin
- encouraged to be imaginative and inventive and brave in their choice of the medium in which they will work
- given the opportunity to apply past experience to their new work
- encouraged to share their ideas with their peer group
- encouraged to be self-critical
- trusted so that they feel able to employ their own ideas and yet remain open to the ideas of others
- encouraged by the knowledge that their work will be respected and stored/displayed with thought and care
- encouraged to demonstrate what they know in different ways
- encouraged to meet and to talk to artists, writers and crafts people
  – in school
  – in the artists' places of work
- taken on a regular basis to museums, dramatic presentations, concerts, zoo, festivals, countryside, places of local interest?

The creative classroom is a place of corporate exploration. To his or her classroom, each teacher brings sympathetic understanding of the difficulties which creating anything entails, an awareness of each child's gifts and potential and a willingness and ability to exercise thoughtful criticism. Quality does not 'just happen'. It comes as a consequence of supporting children in the struggle they have to present ideas in words, sounds, line, colour and movement.

The creative dimension

Written work

The extracts below have been chosen because they are typical of what we should expect and not because they represent work of exceptional quality. They have been reproduced in the form in which they were presented to the teacher.

Examples of children's written work

Make up a story about the sum 4 lots of 12
One day there were 12 children and each child had four sweets each. If all the children put there sweets in one pile there would be 48 sweets altogether. 4 lots of 12 make 48. *Alexander (aged six)*

The suns's a long way away
If a plane went to the sun and travelled at 600 miles in an hour it would take 18 years to get there, as it is the plane would melt before it got there. *Abigail (aged six)*

The workmen
The men are hammering the wall. they were lying on their side. On the concrete. Mr White said there is going to be a dark room and a quiet room with two comfortable chairs. Eric has put up a window. he put up a scree (screen) to stop the dust flying all over the place. *Sari (aged six)*

Louise and I went to look at what was going on and we saw some ws on the windows and eric said it was so that people will not go through because it is glass. they have put some concrete on the ground and a workman called melyn said that ws was for windows. *Juliet (aged six)*

Making a kite
We made an indoor kite. This is how I made it. First we had some tissue paper and then I drew round another kite shape. and then I got some pieces of wire and stuck the wire onto the tissue paper and made a tail. I stuck it on. I got a paper clip and thread and tied it to the kite flier. *Jessica (aged seven)*

Night
I was walking down the street,
The night was rather dark,
I thought I heard a scream,

But it was the wind coming past.
The flowers bent their heads
Night falls fast
We go to our beds
Until night has passed.   *Peter (aged seven)*

A stormy night
On a stormy night
I am a sea gull
Pushed away
Over a roaring sea   *Jack (aged six)*

Easter
When Mary walked in the garden
She saw the lillies weeping
She listened to the birds
In the lonely bare trees.
When Mary walked in the garden
She saw the lillies fair
Glad to know that HE was there.   *Alice (aged six)*

At the science museum
I saw a thing. well. I can't really describe it. it was a round metal ball and when you press the button and put your forehead against the metal ball your hair goes up because of the electricity.   *Tipu (aged six)*

Multi rabbit
'Puff the magic dragon lived by the sea', I sang. Then I found myself singing 'Puff, the multi-rabbit.' I found myself looking into the eyes of a creature.
'I AM THE MULTI-RABBIT', it said. I fell down.
When I regained myself we were in a different place. 'Where am I?'
'On the planet Krypton', said the multi-rabbit. 'It is going to explode.'
Just then it DID.
We found ourselves in 2002, a time odyssey.
But the spaceship did get back to earth.   *Aidan (aged seven)*

7 Being a teacher

Focus on the journey, not the destination. PROFESSOR LEONE BURTON (1993)

Each chapter in this book is united by a common theme: the proposition that, to be successful, the teacher must be aware of the individuality of each pupil. In other words learning is a personal process which takes place within every human being. This process is not determined by age (my five-year-old granddaughter knows many useful things which I do not know); it is not bound by time (the number of hours spent learning how to drive does not make one a good or bad driver) and it cannot be encapsulated within a particular model or teaching style.

Figure 7.1 Learning outside the classroom on a National Trust Estate

Starting school: the vital years

It is the complexity of the learning process which makes teaching so difficult. Our five, six and seven-year-olds are continuously learning – at different speeds, in different places, at different times, through different media and from different people. This complexity forces us as educationalists to look for a standardised approach, a model that will give us security and a sense of direction and purpose. Yet conformity

Figure 7.2 Learning outside the classroom in the British Museum

(achieved through curriculum documents, timetables allocating hours per week per subject) inevitably produces a mismatch. Neither the teacher nor the pupils fit easily into such an 'industrialised' model.

Teaching is a lonely process. After years of training, the young teacher is imprisoned in one room with a group of bright-eyed, lively, young learners. This group have to be met day upon day, week upon week, month upon month. It is very easy in such circumstances, to become educationally sterile, to lose one's vision, to regard work as a continual struggle, like walking up a down escalator.

Working with young children makes considerable demands. The way in which children begin their school-days can determine their attitude to learning for ever. The demands made upon us include not only simply the everyday ones of teaching, caring for and responding to children but also the far subtler demands of self-evaluation and self-criticism.

I was recently invited to observe a group of teachers who were working with children aged between five and seven. The task was straightforward. How could we improve classroom performance? Each of us began, individually, to examine the school day, noting down moments of success, frustration, misunderstanding and unhappiness both inside and outside the classroom. We tried to focus upon those elements which seemed to contribute to an effective learning programme; elements which were in each teacher's control. In the discussions which followed, certain key issues were identified and are summarised below. The questions which emerged provide a useful pattern for personal analysis.

Improving classroom performance

The curriculum

Direction
- Does the way I implement the curriculum recognise that to be effective I must relate it to the needs of each young learner?
- Does it recognise that each child in my care begins the learning process from a different starting point; is possessed of a different pace of understanding and (therefore) needs to focus upon a personal, *attainable* goal?

  The personal goal of Jake (aged six) might be to reach the end of his basic reading text by Friday, that of Sue, who sits next to him, to read her third Astrid Lindgren story within a week.

A number of research projects have pin-pointed causes for disenchantment with schooling. All suggest that a principal cause for such disenchantment is the failure to set children tasks which are appropriate to their abilities. Too often the challenge is poorly directed. It is vital therefore to identify *at as early a stage as is possible* those children who are gifted or who have special needs of any kind.

Some needs are obvious. A six-year-old in a wheelchair requires a suitably designed toilet, ramps and a lift. When the needs are hidden (as in the case of a budding mathematician, a gifted musician or a competent computer user) they can be much more difficult to identify. Children with outstanding abilities deserve to have their gifts recognised. The gifted child, whose potential is ignored, often becomes unhappy and such unhappiness often leads to boredom, frustration and, eventually, to disruptive behaviour.

Approaches
- Do I use a range of different approaches when I present information and ideas?
- Do I use books, charts, wall displays, computer and video programmes in such a way as to involve children as individuals and in small groups – as well as members of a class?

Seven-year-old Mary is fascinated with the wildlife she sees when she wanders through the woods; the picture on page 5 of a class text book leaves her uninterested and disengaged. This all too common example prompts the following question:
- Have I included in each working day opportunities for children to learn through real experiences, through looking, through reflection, through experiment?*

Comprehensibility
- Is the programme which the children are following comprehensible to them? Why is the particular activity being undertaken?
- Does it have a *perceived* purpose?

Young children benefit from being set short-term goals. They do not

---

* These four elements have been classified by David A. Kolb of The Massachusetts Institute of Technology as: concrete experience (feeling), reflective observation (watching), abstract conceptualisation (thinking) and active experimentation (doing).

see themselves as learning for life because they are alive *now*. It is the journey and its unfolding that is of supreme importance, not the final destination.

Integration
Is the programme comprehensive and does it allow for a cross curriculum approach to learning?
- Am I devoting too much time and effort upon narrow subject skills, such as letter formation and addition, or am I teaching these skills within a more creative and wide ranging programme?

Sums, writing practice and colouring in sections of photocopied sheets are an inadequate diet for the growing mind. Six and seven-year-olds thirst for knowledge and understanding. Their interests are unbounded and not restricted by adult-determined academic barriers.

Time

- How do I use time within the classroom?
- How can I use it more effectively?
- Does time shape all that I do or am I sufficiently flexible to allow children to use time expansively?

Very few activities fit neatly into a 45 minute time slot. By giving time to children we help them to understand that time is simply the space we need to complete an activity. Looked at in this way, the activity determines the time, not time the activity. Effective 'timetabling' gives children space to finish whatever task they have begun; be it painting, reading, writing, mathematics or technology.

My description of time as 'learning-space' may seem, at first, confusing. My choice of words is deliberate. Learning cannot be trapped and delivered in timetabled packets. Abstract ideas are not acquired by six or seven-year-olds in one lesson, one week, or one month. Conceptual development grows imperceptibly – over years.

Organisation

- Does the organisation of time and space allow me to work with children:
    as a class
    as groups within the class
    as individuals?

- Am I able to work across these groups regularly and with ease? If not, how might I adjust the timetable and/or the teaching space to enable me to do so?

Independence is a characteristic of five and six-year-olds. Although they like to work alone on individual activities they enjoy doing them in the company of other children. While accepting the paradox of individuality within a group setting, it is important to encourage the move from egocentricity to social co-operation, from responsibility for and involvement in self to care and awareness of others.

It might be that activities which encourage working together are deliberately introduced. It is almost impossible, for example, to create a puppet play without considerable co-operation – the puppets have to be made, the theatre built, the stage properties created, the story chosen and rehearsals undertaken before the play can be presented.

Most important of all, we have to persuade the children that the classroom is *theirs* as well as ours (that is the teacher's). The realisation by each child that he or she is an 'owner' of the room and of all the things in it encourages the development of responsibility and 'shared care'.

Personal reflections

The issues raised above concentrate upon the teacher within a classroom setting. The group of teachers with whom I was working found themselves continually returning to personal awareness, and professional insight.

This self-examination threw up many questions, the most significant of which are included below:

- What do I believe this group of children need of me?
  - What are my expectations?
  - What should my priorities be for them – as individuals, as a class?

- How well do I know the children, their individual and particular strengths and weaknesses?
  - How accurately, *without using standardised tests*, can I 'grade' the children for whom I am responsible in terms of their competence in reading, writing, mathematical understanding, presentation skills, creativity, logical thinking, oralcy, social awareness, ability to concentrate …?
  - What steps am I taking to get to know my children better?

- What links have I established with their parents and with professionals who have previously worked with the children (such as pre-school playgroup leaders, their previous teachers)?
- How carefully do I listen to what they tell me?

- How critical am I of myself?
  - Do I attempt to measure whether I have grown as a teacher since last year?
  - Am I, four months into a school year with a group of teachers new to school, a more secure teacher than I was when I started the term?
  - On what basis am I measuring this growth?

- How caring am I for the classroom environment?
  - Am I sufficiently aware of the visual impact of the room?
  - Am I using the classroom walls to deepen and challenge the children's understanding?

- How do my own beliefs, experiences and personal prejudices affect me as a teacher?
  - Have I clear philosophy which shapes my work.
  - What do I *really* believe?

- In what aspects of teaching and classroom management am I most secure – and most frail?
  - How can I build upon my strengths and improve my weaknesses – by reading, attending courses, talking to more experienced colleagues, visiting other schools?

- What impact am I having on these children?
  - Do the children regard me as someone who is fair, humorous, caring, responsible, well organised, as someone who has time? In less flattering ways, or not at all?

- Do I build into my day sufficient time to observe the children in my care, to try to pin-point what motivates them as individuals, the tensions which shape their behaviour and personality?
  - Do I give myself sufficient time to check progress?
  - Do I know that each child goes home each day with the feeling 'It was good in school today because …'?

- How well do I give children a feeling of physical, social, emotional and intellectual security?

Record keeping

- In what ways might I record children's progress?

The following examples indicate some different ways of keeping records. Taken together with written records (see below) and children's portfolios, they provide a useful and detailed analysis of progress. A portfolio consists of selected examples of each child's work in mathematics, writing, handwriting and drawing. This work, selected every three months and date stamped, provides an excellent guide to progress. Observations made by the class teacher about specific areas of difficulty or success can be attached to the portfolio. The portfolio, which follows the child from teacher to teacher and moves with the child on transfer to a junior department (years three to six), gives a valuable 'thumbnail sketch' of achievement and development. In some schools children are encouraged to review these personal portfolios, enabling each child to validate their own progress. A letter (dated 4 November 1993) to headteachers from the School Curriculum Assessment Authority (SCAA), signed by the Chief Inspectors of Schools for England and for Wales and Sir Ron Dearing, Chairman of SCAA, contained the following statement, 'How teachers record pupils progress is a professional matter for schools to decide .... One approach which schools might like to consider (is) the development of a school portfolio .... This approach would be equally valid at all key stages.'

Specimen record sheets

```
Sheet 1   Number/Mathematics

         Numbers up to 9

Name..................              Date Achieved

Can show a set of objects, recognise,
say and write symbols for 1-9 when
given in any order                  ............

Understands 'more than', 'less than'
and 'equal to' to two sets of objects
no matter how they are arranged     ............

Understands the symbol  =           ............

Can say and write the numbers 1-9
in numerical order
      ascending                     ............
      descending                    ............

Can write dictated numbers 1-9      ............
```

The sheet above is designed to record the attainment of children new to school. Subsequent sheets would follow – relating specifically to tasks and activities which the teacher has set.

A similar sheet could be produced for writing and oracy.

Sheet 1 Language

Name.................   Date Achieved

Can trace letters A-Z   ....

Can trace numbers 0-9   ....

Can copy letters and numbers
reasonably accurately   ....

Can listen attentively to a story   ....

Can retell a story   ....

Can tell own story fluently   ....

Shows an interest in books:
    picture books   ....
    information books   ....
    story books   ....
    poetry books   ....

Can write own name   ....

Being a teacher

```
┌─────────────────────────────────────────────────────────────────────┐
│  Reading record                                                     │
│                                                                     │
│  Date (November)              8  9  10  11  12  15  16  17  18  19  │
│                                                                     │
│  Peter (Red reading Book V)   X  X  X  X                            │
│                                                                     │
│  Sandra (Fairy Stories 2)     X  X  X                               │
│                                                                     │
│  John (1st reader)            X  X  X  X                            │
│                                                                     │
│  Mary (3rd reader)          (abs) X     X                           │
│                                                                     │
│  Alec (H.C. Anderson collection)  X                                 │
│                                                                     │
│  Alice (Poetry III)                  X                              │
└─────────────────────────────────────────────────────────────────────┘
```

This record would be kept by the teacher and contain a list of each child in the class together with a note of the book being read. A mark (X) indicates that the child has been heard to read on a particular day *by the teacher or by some other responsible adult*.

Starting school: the vital years

Group activities: Blue group				
Week of	Jan 5	Jan 12	Jan 19	Jan 26
Peter	Floating and sinking experiments	Helping things to Float	What is special about Water?	Water and machines
Sandra E				
John				
Mary				
Robert				
Fred				
Eric				
May				

This sheet is based on the class described in Chapter 5

A similar chart shown below can be produced for *whole class projects*.

	Jan 5	Jan 12	Jan 19	Jan 26
Topic: Glass	Looking at glass objects — drawings	Coloured glass	How glass is made — using information book, pictures, slide presentation	Making a booklet of information and drawings 'All about glass'
Notes: Absent	Peter Fred John		Peter	

It would probably be wise to support these summary records with a personal record sheet of the type illustrated below.

Personal record sheet

Robert (Date of birth 20.3.87)

15.9.92 Robert began school three weeks later than other children in the class. (He was recovering from a broken left arm – he is right-handed.) During his first three weeks he needed a lot of attention. He had had no pre-school experience, his mother preferring home to institutional care.
He has not mixed well with other children in the group – lonely and aggressive when approached

19.10.92 Some progress. Has made friends with Eric and Patrick. They are inseparable.
Some progress in making letter shapes. Enjoys playing with number apparatus. Responds well to art activities – pictures with great splashes of colour. I have put the painting he did today into his personal folder.

17.11.92 During my absence on a training course, Robert proved very difficult. The supply teacher was upset because she could not control him. Tearful and aggressive – just like when he joined us, it seems. Hates change? Demands a regular pattern to his day.

Some four months later (the intervening entries are not reproduced here).

5.3.93 A good week. Robert has read to me three times this week. He is reading simple stories fluently (Red Story Book, pages 1-26) and seems anxious to continue his rapid progress. Still rather an isolate, but is beginning to share equipment more readily than hitherto. Motor control excellent – some outstanding art work this month.

Notice that the jottings on this personal record sheet are not specifically directed at particular subject areas. Rather they are sketches of Robert at a moment in his school career. The observations are things that the teacher feels important, things she wants to remember and may need to be able to recall – perhaps to clarify his behaviour at some later stage of her work with him, perhaps to share with a colleague when he moves into her class.

It must be stressed that a teacher keeping personal records of this kind does not record every child's doings for every week of the school year. Out of a class of 28 children, only the records of five or six children are written up during any one week. Six sentences written about one child on one day is not too demanding!

The approach to record keeping that I have outlined is supplementary to that implicit in the delivery of the National Curriculum. However record keeping by each teacher in a style and form which he or she

	Addition (to 10)	Addition (to 20)	Subtraction (to 10)	Counting in 5s
Abdul S	•			
Daryl	\	•		
Isata	X	X	\	
Jake	X	X	X	\
Peter	\	•		
Sharon	X	X	X	X
Wahida	\	•		

Key • activity/concept introduced
     \ activity/concept used correctly
     X activity/concept used correctly and with confidence over time

Such a table could be produced for every curriculum area.

uses confidently is a vital complement to those required by statute. Let me therefore include some ideas on how record keeping can encompass teaching requirements that are common to all schools.

Record keeping

Bearing in mind that since the implementation of the *Education Reform Act* of 1988, assessment has come to be used as a tool to measure teacher performance as much as pupil attainment, there is a danger that record keeping is seen only in terms of narrow check lists against given criteria. Such assessment can become arid and worthless – for the value of a child is far more than a series of ticks on a photocopied sheet; 'progress' is something far deeper than the ability to jump through prescribed hoops.

As we have seen above, there have been a number of recent attempts to design learning records that enable teachers to record a child's progress in detail whilst being neither time consuming nor over complex. The Centre for Language in Primary Education (CLPE) in the London Borough of Southwark developed widely used proformas designed to help teachers to keep a diary of comments on each child in their care. Space was given on the forms for diary-like comments on such things as:

- languages understood and spoken
- languages read and written
- names of teachers who work with the child
- a record of significant discussions that have taken place between teacher, parent and child
- achievements in talking and listening, reading and writing
- progress/activities in mathematics and science as well as in the foundation subjects of art, geography, history, music, technology, PE and religious education.

Teachers who have used these (and similar proformas) have assured me that the forms were helpful and simple to keep. A particularly valuable aspect of the CLPE proformas was that spaces were provided in which the teacher could write suggestions of ways in which the child might be helped in future years, and for parents and children to comment upon how they felt about the academic year which had just been completed.

The many changes which have occurred during the short space of time between the conception of the National Curriculum and its implementation make it impossible to include in these pages more than a skeleton of ideas. It is far more effective for each teacher to develop a personal style of record keeping and for each school staff to design their own overall record sheet than to rely upon externally designed models (see also Appendix).

Although record keeping must involve what has happened in the classroom and the children's responses to the activities undertaken, it should also feature a 'teaching projection' or forecast of what might be attempted in the immediate future. Again such forecasts are built around each curriculum area and give the opportunity to establish links across curriculum areas. By planning in advance, it becomes possible to take into account all available resources, to prepare material and to draw upon the expertise of colleagues. If, for example, children are to be introduced to the use of maps, forecasting might involve:

- determining the composition of the groups in which children are to work
- making arrangements with parent helpers or school ancillary staff to take groups to and from local supermarket on local walk
- preparing map(s) of area
- establishing map/atlas/globe display on table in classroom
- obtaining compass(es) for children to handle/discuss
- deciding upon various ways in which children can record experience – on tape, written description, map?
- extending activity. Naming features of local area. Choosing words to describe the local environment
- choosing poetry/songs about shops and shopping
- selecting a folk story about a medieval fair. (The pig who wouldn't come home from market?)
- determining how/whether to introduce children to the idea of co-ordinates and scale
- planning other mapping ideas – from the classroom to the school hall, library, toilets or playground.

Such a forecast provides one of a number of academic 'threads' that are to run through the next month. It is important to realise, however, that a forecast is merely the skeleton of an idea. Fleshed out and activated the theme might last six to eight weeks – or it might fade within two. A degree of flexibility in planning and in the implementation plans is essential when working with young children (see Appendix).

Children's personal records

My record by . . . (Peter)

Week beginning 26 April

I have marked with a ✓ the things I have done today.

	M	T	W	Th	Fr
Reading	✓	✓	✓	✓	✓
Writing	✓	✓	✓	✓	✓
Handwriting practice		✓		✓	
Measuring					
Weighing					
Shapes	✓		✓		
Number		✓		✓	✓
Sand/Water					
Topic (the woods)		✓		✓	
Painting					
Model making	✓				
Free choice			✓		
Cooking			✓		
Music/singing					
Physical education	✓	✓	✓		
Dance				✓	

Friday 30 April
These are things I have to finish next week:
Best copy of my poem
Model of truck
Maths - pages 6 and 7
Sewing
Topic work

As children approach the age of seven they could be encouraged to keep a record of the activities undertaken during a school day. To enable them to do this a 'child's' record sheet will need to be prepared. When photocopied a supply can be made available in a conveniently placed box or tray. As the day progresses, each child marks up his or her sheet. At the end of each week, the sheet is pasted in to a file kept by each child for the purpose.

Responsibility for making a personal analysis of the classroom is central to a teacher's professionalism. It is an important task for teachers, regardless of the age group with whom they are working. Organising a classroom and teaching six and seven-year-olds does, however, make singular demands. For an adult to work alone alongside a class of six-year-olds is often thought to be a lonely and time-consuming occupation. Yet it need not be so.

Sharing experience

The most successful schools that I have visited have a common and identifiable element – the teachers who work in them share their professionalism, their ideas and their plans with their colleagues. This may result in teachers in neighbouring classrooms bringing their classes together to work on some common topic for part of a day; it might be that, in consequence of such a shared experience, they begin to integrate ever more substantial areas of their work and come to regard 60 children as their group, rather than a smaller unit of 30. When such things happen, the adult does not feel so alone for problems can be talked through and skills and expertise shared.

The coming together of teachers to support each other serves as a signpost for much wider areas of co-operation. When young children are admitted to their school, all teachers have a positive part to play. Their support will show itself in many ways. There will be a *staff awareness* that teachers of young children require skills and knowledge every bit as complex and profound as that which is required to teach 16-year-olds or prepare 18-year-olds for university. They will be aware that how well (or badly) children learn during their early years has a significant effect upon their subsequent schooling. They will appreciate that sound management of resources does sometimes mean that the youngest children in the school will receive proportionally more finance than that allocated to children in years 5 and 6. There will, in short, be an acceptance by the whole teaching body that harmony and the search for a common goal are more likely to achieve success than competition and division.

Every school develops its own 'ethos' (climate). Children quickly learn the unspoken rules and the unwritten behaviour patterns of the school they join. The task of all teachers (not just those responsible for the five, six and seven-year-olds) is to ensure that, when children are new to school, they enter a supportive, happy, well-organised, learning community.

The moral climate

In the debate about morality and standards that followed upon the murder, in February 1993, of James Bulger by two ten-year-old boys, the importance of the moral climate within society as a whole was rightly emphasised. Most of these discussions seem to have ignored a key issue. Effective learning occurs in schools in which both teachers and pupils are relaxed, yet feel confident to meet the intellectual and social demands of each new day, and where children are free to express their ideas, in creative ways, knowing that their efforts will be sympathetically and honestly received. In such schools, the organisation of the classroom and of the day will be such as confirms each child's growing confidence and awareness of his or her personal progress. In such a climate, success is not measured against an arbitrary, externally devised formula such as a set of test results or a series of ticks on a duplicated sheet.

Sadly, effective classroom practice is in the process of being drowned in a sea of documentation. When the flutter of papers is finally still, there will be even less time for the classroom to be a place where the most important aspects of the education process are continually emphasised: compassion, care for others, personal responsibility, integrity, self-respect, empathy and honesty. I am not suggesting that such qualities are only taught in schools. They are acquired from parents and from the wider society outside the home. Nevertheless, at a time when the churches command the support of a small minority of the population, the value of school as a place where such qualities can be nurtured has become ever more important.

My personal observations suggest that the recent emphasis upon measurement against rigid external criteria, school league tables and testing has tended to divert teachers from giving as much time as they had done hitherto to those quiet moments of togetherness in which elements central to young children's lives are shared (news about Grandma in hospital, the death of a family pet, a visit to the cinema or a birthday party at a burger house). As an experienced infant head teacher observed to me, somewhat sadly, 'I spend so much time in my room nowadays, I hardly know my children. I feel ashamed to call myself headteacher – because I rarely find time to teach.'

The head who shared these views with me also pointed to another significant change. 'We have new words now, the language of the market place.' Implicit in the way we use words and in the very words we choose to use, is a message. Schools are managed, the curriculum delivered, assessment schemes are validated. Words like audit, inspectors, competition, marketing, evaluation have been introduced to create an image of tough, commercial discipline to institutions whose task is not to market goods but to watch over the intellectual, social and emotional development and well being of young people.

A balance between care and market place has not yet been achieved. Of course teachers must be judged by their successes and their failures. Parents have the right to know how well their children are achieving in school and have the opportunity to take action when schools fail.

If the early years at school result in the demoralisation of children (perhaps by being offered a tedious, undemanding programme or by being made to feel that marks are more important than people) the foundations are laid for subsequent disenchantment with everything that the schools represent.

8 The parental community

Understand my parenting and you will better understand my child. A mother talking to a social worker, South Bronx, New York, June 1975

Tony, Laura and Hilda come to school from a family. Each of their families (whatever their size or composition) mould the children in a unique way. Like children, no two families are alike. Each family provides an individual climate in which children live and grow. Each family gives messages, hidden and overt about the things which are important in life, about social values, about expectations. Tony, Laura and Hilda see their parents reading books (or not); smoking and drinking (or not); quarrelling or living peaceably; being selfish or sharing; listening to classical music, folk or pop (or ignoring music altogether); they observe, often subconsciously, what the adults in their world talk about – social issues, politics, their work, the state of English football, horse racing and the pools or the latest television soap. When they go out and about with their parents they receive a similar range of messages; the comparative value of fishing, visiting museums or sunbathing; the way to behave when with friends or the value of patience when shopping.

Family values

The interaction of child with child, parent with parent or parent with child in a family, lays down *from birth* the values that every child will make his or her own by synthesis and adaptation. If using books is a common-place activity in a home, then the children who grow up in it are the more likely to value books. Conversely if books are a rarity, then children who live and grow alongside non-book users are much less likely to appreciate their value.

This may seem too obvious a point to make, yet my experience suggests that we are sometimes forgetful that each child brings to school a value-system which is shaped, and *continues* to be shaped, by his or her family. These family-inspired values are not necessarily those which complement the values of the school or of the class teacher. Indeed the two sets of values may, in some areas, be in conflict. A child, who continually hears extreme racist propaganda in the home, is not likely to be greatly influenced by the tolerant views he hears advanced in school; a child whose parents follow a fundamentalist religious creed is more likely to be puzzled by the ideas of her teacher than to change the beliefs she lives with at home. This merely confirms the point made with stark simplicity in the well-known saying attributed to the Jesuits: 'Give me a child for the first seven years and you may do what you like with him afterwards.'

The implications of the tensions that a clash of values may cause are far reaching. However many hours Tony may spend in school in any one year, he is influenced for many more hours by the environment of home and street. Without wishing to sound fatalistic, our influence as teachers is minimal. Of course we can encourage Laura to take a book home to read but if Laura's mother and father show little interest in Laura, and even less in the book she is clutching, the effort is in vain.

Herein lies a key to progress. Learning in all its manifestations (academic progress, moral and social development) is most effective when home and school work in harmony. The partnership, however, is not one of equality. As teachers, we can work alongside parents but we should never assume that we occupy the prime position. Our values, our intentions, our dreams for Laura and Hilda remain dreams unless they are given substance and credibility by their parents.

Home and school

It follows, therefore, that when welcoming young children to school, we have first to establish and then sustain a relationship with parents that appreciates this inequality of influence. In accepting this, we acknowledge that, however well we think we know the children in our care, their parents know them better.

Within this uneven partnership lies a hidden strand – the perception of the child and the value system which is growing within him or her. Children quickly become aware that some aspects of family life are best concealed from school. An example, drawn from my own teaching, will serve to illustrate this point. The day after Monica's dad attacked her mother with a carving knife and was taken into police custody, Monica and her mother 'disappeared'. Returning to school some six weeks later, Monica told me that 'she'd been away'. It was only when the case came to court that Monica's absence was explained. To quote her mother, 'I kept her away. We didn't want talk in school. We've got our pride to think about.'

This is a dramatic example, but family issues do not have to be as theatrical as the one I have used to point to the need which parent and child have to protect their family. The 'barrier' is often revealed through the bizarre conversations which characterise many a parent-teacher meeting: 'Are we really talking about the same child? At school Hilda is so quiet and reserved … you are implying that at home things are so different?' Tony who, his father assures us, is the best of children at home may be a most difficult six-year-old to cope with in the classroom.

In suggesting that parental influence is dominant, powerful and pervasive, I am not identifying a new phenomenon. In every society, the pull of home and family has been a driving force in the education of young people. As teachers, we could try to ignore reality and pretend that school values can override those of the family. A wiser course of action might be to adopt a complementary approach.

Children come from many different types of family. What can we do, as school staff, to give support to each child and each family as and when it is needed?

Children hear their parents talking about starting school; they listen to conversations which suggest that life (for their parents) will be a little different when autumn comes; wonder (perhaps suspiciously) at stories they have been told about school and teachers. Even in a small village community, where everybody seems to know everybody else, what *actually* happens within the school walls is a secret known only to those who are taking part. Listen to young children discussing a school day, or talking about their teacher, or describing the moment when the headteacher came into their classroom with an African in traditional dress, and you wonder why your own school days never seemed so frightening – or exotic!

Schools in every community I have visited (from Hong Kong to Calgary) are rich in legends and even the most conventional school will benefit from demystification. This process of explaining, describing and presenting school to people who live in the locality has to be initiated from within. It is the school that should make contact with the community it has been created to serve.

Establishing links with pre-school children

There are a number of ways in which links with pre-school children and their families can be developed.

The first and most obvious way is to encourage an on-going dialogue between the staff of the school (the head, the deputy, the reception teacher) and the pre-school playgroups and nursery units which feed the school.

Links established between the institutions will encourage all those involved in preparing children for school to meet informally. Playgroup personnel will feel able to come into the classrooms into which their children are to move, thus having the opportunity to acquire insights that will help ease the tensions of transfer. At the same time, teachers can be given time to visit the 'feeder' institutions – where they too will hopefully learn something of the children for whom they will ultimately become responsible.

The interchange of adults will result in the exchange of information about the children in whom both groups have a professional interest. When, as headteacher, I established such links, I sought to put them on a formal basis. Roger, an experienced teacher of four to seven-year-olds, spent every Friday morning in a local nursery school. In the course of these visits, he came to know the teachers and how they organised the day. More importantly, from my point of view (as headteacher of the receiving school), he came to know the children through helping them to paint and draw, by telling them stories and by listening to them read and talk. When these children joined primary school, a degree of harmony had already been established between one of my staff and pupils new to school. Although Roger could not possibly have all these newcomers in his class, he had perceptions about Tom or Harriet that he could share with the teachers who were responsible for them once they were admitted.

The coming together of teachers was further developed through visits to the school by pre-school children. They came once a week to join in the school programme: physical education classes, story times, music and movement and lunch. The idea was to familiarise them with the range of activities they would meet in a school week and to help them discover that, although the school building was large, it was possible for them to find their way around it. Their weekly visits enabled teachers, the school secretary and the school keeper to become 'familiar faces'. The children realised that there would be a place in the organisation for them and, in consequence, that starting school was something to anticipate with pleasure.

Links with parents of pre-school children

Such initiation to full-time schooling through established links between institutions is effective, but although it bridges the gap for children it does little for their parents.

The second thrust in any school-home initiative, therefore, needs to be directed at parents. Most schools are in a position to identify the children who are to eventually join them. As in the example given above, it will rest upon the school to seize the initiative and encourage parents to visit school before their child enters full-time schooling.

Using my own professional work as an example, I tried to establish home-school links some two years prior to a child's admission. Once a parent had registered a child we gave him or her the following information sheet shown on pages 100–101.

The implementation of a 'drop in' scheme meant that the teachers were prepared to have an unexpected child (and a parent) sitting in our room to listen to a story, watching a mathematics activity, coming to lunch. The purpose of our strategy was consciously to confirm that school was open to parent and child and by presenting an accurate picture of contemporary schooling, to replace feelings of anxiety with ones of security.

This is to suggest that it is as important to prepare parents to be parents of school children as it is to prepare their children to be pupils in school. Parents continue to bring to school the anxieties about schools and teachers that they had when they themselves were children. For many parents, teachers remain authority figures and schools formidable places. This remains the most difficult barrier for teachers to break down. We may not see ourselves as figures in authority and yet how we greet parents, how we listen to their concerns, even how we stand carries a message – a message which either comforts or confronts. Norman Thomas, a former HMI makes this point most eloquently in a report he prepared for ILEA. He quotes a Bengali mother who said, 'You do not need to speak the language to know whether or not you are welcome.'

The initiatives described above can be supported by adding future parents to school mailing lists; a straightforward thing to do since

Getting ready for school

General points

1 Bring your child to school before full-time schooling begins. We do not have a set plan for parents to follow – but a rough guide would be for children to be brought to school at least 12 times in the term before the age of five and on half-a-dozen occasions before this. This visit need not be a long one – half-an-hour is often sufficient for a four and a half-year-old. Stay with your child so that it is understood that school is not a place which separates children from their parents. Remember to visit during morning and afternoon sessions so that your child can have a variety of school experiences (stories, playing with structural apparatus, PE and so on).

2 Try to make sure that your child knows his way to and from school and can cope with the roads.

3 Try to make sure that your child can accurately give his or her name, address and telephone number.

Practical points

It would be helpful if all children coming new to school could do the following things:
- put on shoes
- dress and undress
- remove outdoor clothes and hang them on a hanger
- use a knife and fork
- use the toilet properly
- wash and dry hands and face efficiently
- tidy up after using toys, apparatus and books.

All these points are, of course, aspects of social training that are as vital to parents as to teachers.

Further suggestions

1 Include your child in adult conversations whenever practical. Never talk down to your child. Discuss arrangements for shopping, holidays and trips. Watch television together and discuss the programme items.

2 Read to your child – every day, if possible. Take your child to the public library and encourage him or her to look at books.

3 Make scrap books with pictures. Print relevant words beneath each picture. *Never* print in capitals. These scrap books may then be used as simple reading books.

> **4** Encourage your child to paint, crayon, cook – activities that give opportunity for conversation and increase confidence.
>
> **5** Play games with your child which encourage counting or recognition of shapes, such as Ludo, Snakes and Ladders, Snap or jigsaw puzzles.
>
> **6** Help your child to realise how numbers occur in life – not by doing sums but by counting various things, for example, how many forks are on the table and how many cars are there in the road? Number rhymes and songs are also a great help.
>
> If you have any worries about your child starting school please discuss your concerns with a member of the school staff.

most school offices are equipped with computers. Such mailing shots might include a copy of the school magazine, the school profile, a home-school or PTA newsletter, invitations to open days, school plays and concerts. Not all future parents will attend all or any of these events, but the very decision to write carries an unequivocal message: 'This is what our school is about. You are part of our school. You are welcome to share it with us.'

Such commitment requires resourcing and will take time to establish itself. Once established, the importance of 'valuing parents' will become apparent. In all the schools in which I have worked, since 1954, a very real attempt was made to involve parents in their children's schooling. In all of them – in poor, inner-city districts and in the more prosperous suburbs – I found parents willing to help enrich the life of the school. This enrichment might be quite ordinary, like repairing a rabbit hutch or caring for the classroom pets over a long holiday. It might be time consuming, like accompanying a teacher on a class visit or helping repair library books. It might be mundane, like cleaning art and craft equipment at the end of the school year; or extremely creative, like designing and making costumes for a school play.

Sometimes this 'coming to help' was initiated by the school, sometimes it reflected a personal adult need. 'Could I help with the school garden? I've just moved into a flat and I've nowhere to grow flowers.' This latter example indicates, I suspect, that parents also have needs which a school can help satisfy. In this context it is significant that, if parents find the school a comfortable place to be, then the children in the family will be given very positive messages about it.

Removing barriers between home and school brings many other advantages. It eases, for example, talk between teacher and parent. I still remember (and value) the exchange of confidences which took place between me and the parents of children I was employed to teach. 'If James is a bit sad today, it's because his grandpa has gone to hospital'; or 'Keep an eye on Mary tomorrow. I'm having another baby. I've just come from the doctor and I'll tell Mary all about it on the way home tonight'; or again, 'I can't get Mandy to talk this morning. Last evening she saw my brother throw himself from the second-floor bedroom window.'

To teach children effectively, to help them live in school, teachers have to learn to become sensitive listeners.

Parenting is a complex activity and one for which few adults are adequately prepared. Schooling, on the other hand, is something which all parents have experienced and most of them feel they understand. Yet schools of today are not like those of yesterday. Over the past 20 years, there have been considerable changes in educational methodology. Technology (and with it computer use at an ever-earlier age) is occupying a central place in the school programme, mathematics books are being supplemented with all manner of structural apparatus, 'going and doing' is replacing 'sitting and listening'. All of these developments have had the effect of distancing schools from parents; of throwing into confusion all the comfortable assumptions about what happens in a classroom, about school organisation and the ways in which young children learn.

But the distance can be so easily narrowed and the assumptions brought up to date. Modern methodology can be shared with parents.

One way of developing awareness and understanding is through parent's meetings at which parents use the same materials and apparatus as are used by their children. I attended one such meeting. The school hall was filled with tables. On each table there were different types of mathematical equipment – balances, equalisers, number squares, uni-fix cubes and apparatus for measuring time. Some of the apparatus was of a type which one might use with five-year-olds. Other apparatus was appropriate to children of ten, eleven and twelve. Teachers set the parents problems of the kind that their children faced every day. 'You have a single centimetre cube. Hold it in your hand. How many more centimetre cubes will you need to fix onto it to make the next cube in the sequence? And if the cube is

4 × 4 × 4 cm how many centimetre cubes will you need to build it?' After about two hours of mixed, practical mathematical activites, the general reaction of the parents was expressed by the remark of a bank employee. 'I did sums all day but mathematics this evening. I had to think!' This mathematics evening was one of many educational evenings run by the school (focusing on such things as learning to read, computers in school, painting and creative crafts).

The example given in the preceding paragraph illustrates a point which is so easy to overlook. What we teach in the early years is the foundation of what comes after. It is appropriate that the parents of our five, six and seven-year-olds should be helped towards an understanding of 'why we do what we do' with their children.

The programme of home-school links I have outlined is ambitious and places yet another layer of responsibility upon teachers. Yet our

Figure 8.1 Using the skills and expertise of parents

young learner is so vulnerable – to the pressures of home, school and society beyond. This very vulnerability provides a motive for the coming together of teachers, parents and administrators, a motive for creating a school community which truly focuses upon young people within the families in which they live and grow.

Teachers and parents

Some questions for personal reflection.

- Can I recognise and identify the parents of all the children in my class?
- Have I spoken to at least one of the parents of each of the children in my class during the last 8 weeks?
- Whose parent(s) do I need to talk to in the immediate future? How best can I arrange a meeting? Should the meeting be formal or informal?
- When I meet the parent(s) of particular children do my conversations tend to be negative or positive? If they are invariably negative, how can I redress the balance?
- Do I allow myself time to talk to parents when they come to meet children at the end of the school day?
- Have I drawn up a list of parents who are willing to help me
    on day trips?
    on visits?
- Do I give all the parents of children in my class the opportunity to become involved?
- Do I know the parents sufficiently well to invite those with particular skills to help with specific projects in school (for example, computing, craft activities, country dancing)?
- Do I relate to the parents informally as well as formally – or are all my conversations by appointment?
- Do I actively invite parents to visit the classroom and to look at the work of the whole class (not just the work of their own child)?
- Are the parents involved in the children's activities – at home as well as in school?
- Do parents feel at ease with me? (If your response is negative, how could the situation be improved?)
- Do the parents trust the children to my care?
- Do I invite parents to share the successes of the classroom – by inviting them to assemblies, religious festivals, plays and presentations?
- Am I honest in my discussions with parents?
- What steps could I take as an individual teacher within my school setting to further and develop home-school relationships?

9 School and the young child

I try not to let schooling get in the way of my education.   MARK TWAIN (1835–1910)

The age at which children start school varies from society to society and from one historical epoch to the next. On a study visit to Belgrade, I visited an institution for child care that took in children at the age of six months. Like many similar institutions on the sprawling housing estate it served, this centre was built and staffed, with *parents* (not children) as its central concern. The need for a supply of cheap and plentiful female labour motivated the state to provide child-care facilities. Even in developed countries, similar economic forces are at work. In high wage economies, like those of Scandinavia, the depth of pre-school provision is a reflection of high living costs (mothers need to work); high social expectations (such as holidays abroad or the ownership of a country cottage); a firm belief in the economic independence of women and the acceptance of all these elements by government institutions responsible for education, culture and child welfare.

While it may be politically expedient for a whole variety of economic and social reasons to focus upon a particular age for children to begin school there is no agreed pedagogic merit in sending children to full-time schooling either:
- at three (nursery schools in the United Kingdom)
- at five (all children in the United Kingdom)
- at six (as will apply to children in Sweden from 1995)
- at seven (as currently applies to Bulgaria).

Unfortunately bureaucratic considerations prevent us from taking children into school on the basis of individual intellectual, emotional, physical and social development. Even if such aspects could be accurately measured, state laws for education impose standards which rarely allow for flexibility in their interpretation and implementation. So we should approach the idea of school at five, mindful of the reservation that for some children the starting age is ideal, but that for many others it may be too early or too late.

Having noted the administrative straight-jacket that is created by national laws strictly applied and, at the same time, observing that the neat packaging of people by date of birth is a characteristic of all governments, it is obvious that we cannot expect the education service to be exempt from the way in which state provisions are dispensed. That said, we *can* do something to ameliorate some of the more negative impact of state laws upon children.

Mixed-age teaching

One of the most significant developments in educational thought since the 1950s has been a re-evaluation of the practice of placing children in class groups on the basis of the day, month and year of birth.

Mixed-age teaching has its critics as well as its supporters, for it can pose organisational problems for the less experienced teacher. The methodology should not, however, be lightly dismissed. The great advantage of mixed-age (family) grouping is that it facilitates individual learning, encourages independence and allows children to develop and progress at their own pace. Critics accept this but observe that it places too great a demand upon organisational skills and that where a national curriculum is being followed some of its content may become obscured and lost. In response to such an observation, one could well ask what schools should be – places of minimal achievement set against average standards or centres of excellence where children are able to exceed their teacher's, their parents' and even their own expectations.

This conflict of opinion noted, let me now describe how mixed-age group teaching might be initiated in a school which has hitherto been organised on a traditional age-grouped basis. For ease of description, I will assume that a group of six-year-olds have already been in the school for a year and in the coming September will move into Year 1. A new intake of 30 five-year-olds is to join the school in August. This group can be treated as 'reception' class (as was its predecessor) or, instead, two parallel classes could be established. If this were done, each class would consist of 15 five-year-olds and 15 six-year-olds. The six-year-olds in each class have already spent one year in school, and are experienced in its ways. This means that they can provide role models for the younger newcomers and show how to cope with what 'being at school' involves – its privileges, responsibilities and expectations.

In each of the two classes there will be five-year-olds who will quickly show that they are capable of undertaking school tasks alongside their older classmates – and six-year-olds who can be given time to master the skills that eluded them in the previous school year. The two year 'mix' also has other advantages. Children who are older, but socially or emotionally less developed, are placed alongside younger children. This means that their needs can be inconspicuously met. Who will notice six-year-old Ben is playing with building bricks in the company of Martha aged four and three quarters? If five-year-old Jane has an above average writing ability, should she not be given the opportunity to work alongside children who are one year her senior? It is in these subtle, but important, areas of individual competence, argue supporters of mixed-age grouping, that its advantage lies, for it enables teachers to prepare programmes that relate to the real needs of individual children.

Teachers, organising such a classroom, need not feel that the curriculum they are following prevents diversion and experimentation. Using the example of floating and sinking described in Chapter 5 may be an important element in the official science curriculum. If some five-year-olds become engaged in these activities it does not mean that in doing so they have completed the topic and for the rest of their school lives can put it to one side. J.S. Bruner (1976), the American psychologist and educator, suggests that embedded understanding comes from returning again and again to areas of knowledge, each return taking the learner to *a higher level* of understanding. He conceives learning as a continuous spiral of growth, rather than defined boxes of information each set apart from its predecessor.

Bruner's analysis points to the weakness of a school curriculum which is based upon age related targets. We learn, throughout our lives by building upon and extending what we already know, not by being fed snippets of information arbitrarily presented.

The teachers in my imaginary mixed-age class would use the curriculum to take the children forward – in reading, writing, science, mathematics, and social studies – aware that there might be some repetition in the future, but conscious that every topic (even floating and sinking) can be approached and presented in many different ways and at many different intellectual levels.

It is this 'collection of individuals' with their range of interests, enthusiasms and presentational skills who make up a school staff which give children opportunities to develop their own academic and personal strengths. Thinking back to our own school days, we can probably still remember certain teachers who filled us with enthusiasm for school, for a particular subject, or who gave us a new way of approaching our studies. We can probably also recall teachers for whom we had little personal liking but who were deeply respected by our classmates.

Dangers of over-centralisation

When change is introduced into any school system by a government it is often accompanied by a massive administrative bureaucracy. My observations of education practice in the British Isles and in other countries would suggest that, although national and local government must exercise continual oversight to ensure that young people are given all the skills necessary to live successfully in an ever changing world, great care must be taken to avoid administrative over-kill and over-centralisation.

When young children start school the need for a curriculum imposed from central government is minimal. The teacher's tasks, that of leading children into reading for information and pleasure helping them to record; laying down the basics of numeracy and mathematics; enthusing them for knowledge; helping them share and be responsible for others as well as for themselves have been the common goals of generation upon generation of teachers. Such goals are best realised when curriculum planning is delegated to a local level. Ideally it will be left in the control of individual schools, where the staff will be in the best position to identify ways in which the goals, listed above, can be achieved.

School-based local autonomy will allow the organisation of the early years of school to relate directly to the personnel and resources that are available. (We could call this the 'How?' in education.) It will also mean that the curriculum (the 'What?') will be better able to reflect the specific peculiarities of the school and the population it is there to serve. For example, a school located in the centre of an industrial city is likely to demand a slightly different curriculum focus to one situated in a rural village; in areas with large ethnic minorities specific cultural elements will need to be taken into consideration if the curriculum is to be comprehensible and relevant. All communities (and the school is a community) are different – even if they are adjacent. Such differences are the more easily taken into account when a curriculum is locally planned rather than centrally imposed.

A further consideration governing the age at which children transfer from one learning institution to the next, is how well the professionals in the two institutions have come to know each other.

Inter-professional links

Individual schools can so easily become places where 'our' children live 'our' rules in 'our' school. Social institutions stay alive and vibrant when they are courageous enough to open their doors to the outside world. Headteachers and senior staff of schools have an active part to play by providing opportunity for interaction between different institutions to take place. Headteachers who visit and take an active interest in the nursery schools or pre-school playgroups which feed their school give an important message to their staff and to the staff of the institutions they visit. 'I need to know and to understand. In making my visits I come to listen and to learn as well as to make suggestions.' As a former headteacher, I know how easy it is to hide behind paperwork, to use a telephone rather than go to meet a colleague face to face. If my experience is typical, such a *visible* commitment can be time-consuming, but it pays enormous dividends in the future.

Children also deserve to have teachers who have sufficient confidence to liaise closely with other professionals and workers who 'touch' the early years of childhood. Similarly teachers who are school-based need to be given time to visit pre-school playgroups and nurseries. Both groups can give each other support and insight, both groups can assist children through the traumas of transfer. Each group can listen to the concerns of the other. The value of well-established links between educational units that are united by the children that they commonly come to share should never be underestimated.

The teacher's role

Sadly, in many cultures, the teachers of very young children are accorded little respect by their fellow professionals who work with older children, and by the society in which they work. We can do little about the way society devalues the professionalism of those who work with its youngest members but we can help correct the misconception that only minimum skills and little knowledge are required by their teachers.

Everyone values recognition and encouragement and teachers of young children deserve public recognition of the importance of their work and encouragement to continue with it. Unfortunately when the economic climate worsens and spending on educational provision is reduced, it is usually directed at the service provided for the youngest children.

Hopefully one day, somewhere in Europe, the Education Minister of a National Government will be wise enough to say: These young people are our nation's future. We will ensure, above all else, that because the first years in school are so important to each child's future development, we will resource them effectively.

Were such a statement to be made and implemented in our nation, starting school could become the adventure and challenge it ought to be.

Appendix

DRAFT SHEET FOR INITIAL PLANNING

Ideas are consolidated on to the main core planning sheet.

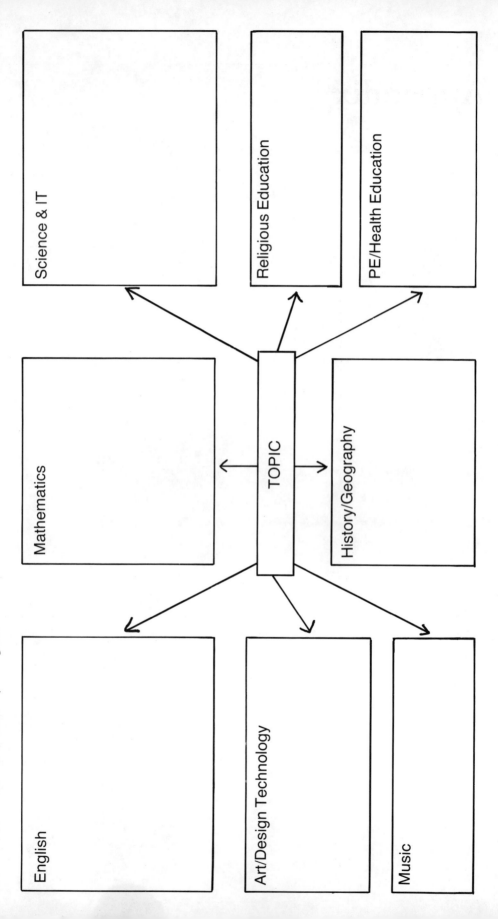

Resources: Books/Library
Audio-visual

Other support required: (e.g. Second Language teacher)
Visits: contact people

TOPIC CORE PLANNING SHEET

Date._____

Aims/Objectives	Resources
Skills	
Concepts	
Information to be covered	
	Audio-visual

English	Maths	Science	
History	DT	Music	RE
Geography	Art	PE	Support staff
			Visits

This sheet is a summary of overall aims and is prepared in advance of the project but can be amended as work progresses.

WEEKLY PROJECT RECORD SHEET

Week beginning _____

English	Mathematics	Science	Resources
History	Geography	Art/Design	Support Staff
Technology	PE/Dance	Music	RE
			Visits

This sheet is written up each week as a record of what actually happened.

Bibliography

Arus, P. 1973. *Centuries of Childhood*. Penguin, London.

Ash, A. 1993. *Days of Grace*. Heinemann, London.

Athey, C. 1990. *Extending thought in Young Children*. Paul Chapman, London.

Bartholomew, L. and Bruce, T. 1993. *Getting to Know You*. Hodder & Stoughton, London.

Barrs, M. and Johnson, G. 1993. *Record Keeping in the Primary School*. Hodder & Stoughton, London.

Blackie, J. 1974. *Changing the Primary School*. MacMillan, London.

Blenkin, G. M. and Kelly, A.V. 1988. *Early Childhood Education – a Developmental Curriculum*. Paul Chapman, London.

Bruce, T. 1987. *Early Childhood Education*. Hodder & Stoughton, London.

Bruner, J. S. 1976. *Play – its role in development and evolution*. Penguin, London.

Bruner, J. S. 1960. *Process in Education*. Knopt Vintage Books, New York and Harvard University Press, Cambridge, Mass.

Cook, C. 1946 (first published 1919). *The Playway*. Harrap, London.

Clegg, A. 1980. *About our Schools*. Basil Blackwell, Oxford.

Clegg, A. 1973. *The Changing Primary School*. Chatto & Windus, London.

Curzon, O. 1985. *Teaching in Further Education*. Holt, Kolb and Fry, New York.

Davies, R. 1983. *The Deptford Trilogy*. Penguin Books, London.

Davies, R. 1989. *The Cornish Trilogy*. Penguin Books, London.

Davies, R. 1991. *The Salterton Trilogy*. Penguin Books, London.

Dewey, J. 1963 (24th Edn). *Experience and Education*. Collier Books, New York.

Dewey, J. 1956. *The Child and Curriculum Change*. University of Chicago Press, Chicago.

Drummond, M. J. 1993. *Assessing Children's Learning*. David Fulton, London.

Edwards, D. and Mercer, N. 1987. *Common Knowledge: The Development of Understanding in the Classroom.* Methuen, London.

Gerber, B. 1977. *Piaget and Knowing.* Routledge & Kegan Paul, London.

Hartley, D. 1993. *Understanding the Nursery School.* Cassell, London.

Isaacs, S. 1967 (first published 1932). *The Children We Teach.* University of London Press, London.

Marsh, L. 1973. *Alongside the Child.* A & C Black, London.
Marshall, S. 1966. *Experiment in Education.* Cambridge University Press, Cambridge.
McCormach Calking, L. 1984. *Lessons from a Child.* Heinemann, London.
Mitchell, C. and Koshy, V. 1993. *Effective Teacher Assessment.* Hodder & Stoughton, London.

Paley, V. G. 1990. *The Boy who would be a Helicopter.* Harvard University Press, Cambridge, Mass.
Pluckrose, H. 1987. *What is happening in our Primary Schools?* Blackwell, Oxford.
Pluckrose, H. 1988. *School – a place for children?* Watts, London.

Tizard, B. et al. 1988. *Young Children at School in the Inner City.* Lawrence Erlbaum Associates, London.

Vigotsky, L. V. 1962. *Thought and Language.* M I T Press, Cambridge, Mass and John Wiley, London.
Vigotsky, L. V. 1978. *Mind and Society.* Harvard University Press, Cambridge, Mass.

Reports

Department of Education and Science. 1966. *Children and their Primary Schools.* HMSO, London.
Department of Education and Science. 1983. *Education 5–9.* HMSO, London.
Department of Education and Science. 1985. *Education for All.* HMSO, London.

Thomas, N. 1985. *Improving Primary Schools*. ILEA, London.

Lord Walton of Detchant. 1993. *Learning to succeed*: Report of National Committee on Education. Heinemann, London.

Index

achievement, feeling of 25
activity changes 51
activity, physical 12–13, 20, 52
age
    and academic ability 7–8
    mixed-age teaching 106–8
    school starting 4–5, 105–6
animism 17
arts, the 30
    see also creative work
Ash, Arthur *Days of Grace* 63
assessment 89
    see also record keeping
Ausubel, David 19

'back to basics' movement 3, 5–6
book weeks 40
books 39–40, 49
'brain map' 32
Brinson, Peter 55
Britton, James 24
Bruner, J.S. 59, 107
Bulgaria 4

caring environment 28
centralization
    dangers of over 108–9
Centre for Language in
    Primary Education (CLPE) 89
challenge, feeling of 25–6
classroom, the
    equipment 35–40, 49, 54–5, 71
    flexible space, 42–4, *43*, 54
    history project example 56–9
    layout 44–5, *44, 47–9, 48*
    use 49–56
Clegg, Sir Alec 28
concrete operational stage
    of thinking 18
Cook, Caldwell *The Playway* 19, 64
core learning 19
creative work 63, *65*

children's written work 73–4
    encouraging creativity 62–73, *66, 68, 69*
    equipment 37–8, 71
curiosity 12–13, 63
curriculum 24–5, 108
    feelings which should be generated by 25–8
    implementation 31–3
    principal components of a programme of tudy 29–31
    teachers and 77–9
    see also National Curriculum for England

Darwin, Charles *Origin of the Species* 16
Davies, Robertson 23
Days of Grace (Ash) 63
Dewey, John (quoted) 67
displays 32, *41*, 42, 49, 57

Education Act 1944 2
Education Reform Act 1988 3, 89
Education through Art (Read) 63
English *see* language
equipment 35–40, 49, 54–5, 71

families 95
    family values 95–6
    see also parents
Field, S. 64
flexible space 42–4, *43*, 54
formal operational stage of thinking 18
Freud, Sigmund 16
Froebel, Frederick (quoted) 19

geography 61
gifted children 78
Gorki, Maxim (quoted) 19

Hadow Reports 1–2
history 60
    project example 56–9

summary of subject links 60–2
History of Mr Polly (Wells) 67
home-base area 47, 49, 54
home-corner 45, 49
   equipment 37

imagination 17
imaginative-play 13–14
   equipment 37
individuality 7–8, 23–4, 27, 35, 75
instruments 38
intellectual development stages 16–18
interest areas 42–4, 45
Isaacs, Susan 13

language 16, 20, 29, 56, 61
layout, classroom 43–5, 43, 47–9, *48*
'learning tree' 32
learning-space 78
listening skills 55

materials 70–1
   see also equipment
mathematics 29, 51, 61–2
   equipment 38–9, 48
measuring 20, 39
mixed-age teaching 106–8
moral climate 93–4
motor play 16
motor-skill development 30
movement 12–14, 20, 52
museums, 20, 70
music 62, *69*
   equipment 38

National Curriculum for England 56, 58, 60–2
   see also curriculum
numbers *see* mathematics
nursery schools 98, 109

operational stage of thinking 18
outside play 52
   equipment 36

parents 95
   family values 95–6
   home and school 96–7
   home-school links 99–104, *102*

patterns, 39
perceptions, a child's 11–12, 17
personal awareness
   teachers and 80–2
personal records 87–8, 89–90
   by children 90–1
physical activity 12–14, 20, 52
Piaget, Jean 16
   analysis of intellectual development 16–17
play 16–20, *50*
   physical 12–13
playgroups 98, 109
Playway, The (Cook) 19, 64
pleasure from learning 25
Plowden Report 1–2
political climate 3, 5–6
portfolios 82
practical skills 30
praise, importance of 55
pre-operational stage of thinking 16–17
pre-school children 98–104, 109
presentation 71–2
   see also displays
Prini, Pietro 24, 33
progress, individual
   record keeping 55

questioning 14–15

Read, Herbert *Education through Art* 63
record keeping 55, 82, 88–91
   specimen record sheets 82–9, 91
resources *see* equipment
responsibilities 20–1
Rupp, George (quoted) 26

safety 21, 27
sand-play equipment 36
Schiller, J.C.F. von (quoted) 19
School Curriculum Assessment
   Authority (SCAA) 82
science 60
security 21, 27
senses, the 11–12, 17
sensorimotor play 16
Shakespeare, William (quoted) 24
social climate 5–6
social skills 20, 30

sorting 38
space, flexible 42–4, *43* 54
Sweden 4

table toys 38
talk, importance of 49, 55
Tanner, Robin 67
teachers 28–9, 75–7
   and the curriculum 77–9
   and the moral climate 93–4
   organisation of time and space 79–80
   personal reflections 80–2
   professional links 98, 109
   record keeping 82–90
   role 109–10
   sharing experience 92–7
   time, 71, 78
   see also classroom
thematic studies 29, 31–3

see also history project example
thinking skills 16–19
Thomas, Norman 101
time
   for creative work 71
   and learning 8
   teachers and 79
tools *see* equipment
trust, feeling of 27

values 95–6

Wayne, John 11
weighing 38–9
Wells, H.G. *The History of Mr Polly* 67
wet activities 44–5, 53
   equipment 36–7
written work 73–4